Ramen Cookbook

The true taste of Japan in your home | Learn how to prepare delicious traditional, vegan and vegetarian recipes for a unique culinary experience!

By Aiko Yamamoto

Table of Contents

Introduction

Welcome to this cookbook completely dedicated to ramen! If you are a lover of this fantastic dish, then you are in the right place. Ramen is a traditional Japanese dish of noodles served in broth, usually accompanied by meat, eggs and vegetables, but that's not all: there are so many variations and customizations that can be made, in fact there are many fish, vegetarian and vegan versions.

It is a perfect dish to be enjoyed in company with friends or the whole family.

There are many different types of ramen, made from the combination of characteristic broths and a wide variety of ingredients. Another key element is the noodles; there are many types, but the ones used for ramen have a real secret ingredient...you'll find out by reading on!

In this cookbook you will find a wide selection of ramen dishes, from classic versions to my own personal creations. There are dishes for every taste, from vegetarian ramen to ramen with pork, chicken or salmon. I have included variations with miso broth, shoyu broth and tonkotsu broth, each with its own unique and distinctive flavor.

There are also more creative ones, but I don't want to anticipate anything, just know that if you really appreciate this dish, and Japanese culture, you will have a great time reading and cooking all the recipes you will find in this book.

I hope they inspire you to experiment and create your own perfect ramen. Don't forget to play around with the ingredients to suit your taste.

Enjoy!

My Life

My name is Aiko Yamamoto and I was born in the small town of Hiraizumi. The town is great and my childhood was happy and carefree. In Hiraizumi, my parents ran a small ramen stand and I, from a very young age, was always fascinated by it. Almost every day I would sit in those wooden chairs and watch the passion with which my parents prepared the broth, noodles and all the ingredients needed to make this fantastic dish.

Of course, as you can imagine, their passion overwhelmed me and I began right away to help them, initially my job was to measure all the ingredients. I had gotten so good at it that I didn't even need the scale anymore!

The older I became the more tasks I was given were numerous, over the years I learned all the secrets of making a perfect noodle, creating a strong tasting broth, but even more importantly, I learned how to balance all the complex flavors found in ramen.

At the age of twenty-five, I began traveling all over Japan, discovering other versions of ramen and learning new cooking techniques. I also participated in several local festivals and was very successful; it is something I am still proud of today.

A few years after my parents retired, I took over the family business and turned it into a real restaurant. When I am not in the kitchen, I am dedicated to promoting ramen culture, both live through classes and by writing books. I am proud of my culture and it makes me happy to share it with others.

Making this book took a long time, I hope I can convey all my passion to you, and I hope that by reading it, you will enjoy it as much as I enjoyed writing it. If you like the content of the book, I ask you to leave me honest feedback, I would really enjoy it!

Where Ramen Came From

Ramen originated in Japan during the Meiji period (1868-1912), when the country began to open its doors to the outside world and began importing ingredients such as wheat and pork from abroad. In the 1950s and 1960s, ramen became even more popular in Japan, and today it is one of the country's most beloved dishes.

It was introduced to Japan by Chinese people working in the country's ports. Initially, it was considered a poor food, eaten mostly by laborers and sailors. However, in the 1950s and 1960s, ramen became increasingly popular and is now one of the country's most beloved dishes.

There are many theories about the origin of the name "ramen." One of them claims that it comes from the Chinese word "lamian," which means "hand-pulled noodle." Another theory holds that the name comes from the Japanese word "ra-men," meaning "wheat vermicelli."

In recent years, ramen has also gained popularity in other countries around the world, becoming an icon of Japanese cuisine.

Ramen Curiosities and Anecdotes

Ramen is a very versatile dish and can be prepared in many different ways. In Japan it is so popular that there are festivals dedicated exclusively to it. One of the most famous is the Sapporo Ramen Festival, held annually in Sapporo, the capital of the island of Hokkaido. At this festival, visitors can taste ramen of all kinds and from all over Japan.

Another way in which ramen has become popular in Japan is through "ramen battles," competitions in which different restaurateurs compete in unique recipes and intense flavors. These challenges have become so popular that they have been televised and have even inspired a manga and anime series.

Ramen has become a global phenomenon, with restaurants serving the dish all over the world. There are even schools where ramen is taught exclusively; there, aspiring chefs can learn how to prepare the broth and noodles to perfection.

Every October 6, Ramen Day is celebrated in Japan. During this holiday, many restaurants and eateries offer special deals and discounts on their ramen noodles, and there are often ramen-themed events and activities around the country. It is a perfect opportunity for ramen enthusiasts to sample different recipes and flavors of this delicious dish.

In 1964, the first ramen restaurant to open in Japan was "Shina Soba," which served a version of the dish called "Chukasoba." However, this restaurant was not very successful and closed only a few months after opening. Soon after, another ramen restaurant called "Taishoken" opened in Yokohama and became very popular, becoming the first truly successful ramen-themed restaurant in Japan.

In 1993, the first ramen restaurant to open in America was "Ramen Tatsunoya," which opened in Gardena, California. Tatsunoya quickly became popular and inspired many other restaurants to open in the United States. Also thanks to it today, there are many ramen restaurants, serving different versions of the dish, from classic tonkotsu to vegan.

In 2010, a man named Kanji Nakatani set the record for the fastest consumption of ramen, eating a whole portion in just 3 minutes and 45 seconds. Nakatani became famous for his skill in the "ramen battles" challenge, in which participants must eat large amounts of ramen as fast as possible. Not only was he able to set this record, but he also won numerous challenges throughout Japan. Today, Nakatani is known as the "ramen king" and continues to participate in similar challenges throughout the country.

Another curious anecdote about this dish: in 2011, the Japanese government launched a campaign to promote it as one of the country's cultural symbols. The campaign, called "The Great Japan Ramen Adventure," invited tourists to visit Japan and try different ramen recipes in all regions of the country. The goal was to showcase the variety and creativity of Japanese ramen and to encourage tourists to discover Japan's culinary treasures. The campaign was a success and helped make ramen even more popular all over the world.

The Basis for a Perfect Ramen: the Broth

One of the basic elements of ramen is undoubtedly the broth. There are hundreds of different recipes; it is a dish that lends itself to many variations and interpretations. Each version, however, always has a solid base from which to start: the broth. Ramen broth is rich, aromatic and flavorful, capable of enveloping all the ingredients and bringing out their individual flavors.

Making a good broth takes hours; the longer it cooks, the better it will taste. Don't worry, you won't have to be constantly there in the kitchen, you can put it on the stove and take a look at it from time to time, you can also prepare it well in advance, in fact, in the refrigerator it can stay up to two days without any problems. You can also freeze it if you wish to keep it longer. I realize that preparing a broth takes time and often, with today's pace, we don't have it. Unlike many other long preparations, however, broth is basically 100% liquid, and this is a great advantage. Remember:

Broth can be stored for a long time in the freezer and, unlike solid foods, can be thawed at the last moment directly in the pot. After a few minutes on the stove, it will look exactly as it was just made.

You'll be able to afford to make the broth even once a fortnight, all you have to do is freeze it divided into portions and you'll have it available whenever you feel like ramen, it will only take a few minutes. Convenient, right?

What if you're in the mood for ramen but just haven't had time to make the broth? Don't worry, there are a couple of recipes in this book that involve quick preparation, allowing you to make them in no time at all. Once you get the hang of the technique you can also make an "express" broth; obviously it won't taste the same as a broth that will have boiled two hours, but it's still a good compromise.

There are four classic Ramen broths. In the first part of this chapter I will explain in detail how to prepare each of them, the preparations are very similar and once ready they will be the basis of your ramen. With the exception of Tonkotsu, where it is "mandatory" to use pork, in the other three you can decide to use meat or fish indifferently. There is no precise rule, personally I prepare them using meat if the final ramen dish will have meat, conversely I use fish if the final ramen dish will have fish among the ingredients.

Small clarification, when I say "pork bones," or "chicken bones" among the broth ingredients, I mean a piece in which both the meat and the bone are present. In this way, the broth will have a much more intense flavor, plus it will be easier to make: for example, you only need to take chicken already cut into pieces (it can be found in any supermarket) and you can use it as is, straight from the package to the pot.

On the other hand, when you use fish, I recommend using only the less noble parts for the broth, such as the heads, bones or carapaces: all the flavor is concentrated there and the resulting broth will be rich and tasty. This way, you can also cook the fish meat separately and use it to make up the final dish, or even set it aside for another recipe.

In the second part of the chapter, to expand the recipes available to you and to open ramen to vegetarian and vegan versions, I have added three more broths, which are simpler and less "traditional," but no less tasty.

Are you ready to cook? Let's get started right away!

Classic Broths

Tonkotsu

The first preparation I want to tell you about is Tonkotsu. This word in Japanese means "pork bone," which is the main ingredient in this thick, white-colored broth. The broth is made by boiling pork bones over a high fire for several hours, resulting in a strong flavor with a creamy, slightly fatty texture. Some recipes call for this broth to be mixed with a certain amount of chicken stock and vegetables. Sometimes ginger is added to the final dish to freshen the mouth a little and give that aromatic note that goes well with Tonkotsu.

This broth needs many hours of cooking, but also a few hours of "rest," so to get a perfect result I recommend that you prepare it a day in advance, but it is not mandatory. Here is how to properly prepare tonkotsu broth for ramen:

Ingredients

7 liters of water
1.5 kg of pork bones, preferably knee
or shoulder bones
50 g kombu seaweed

1 medium onion, cut in half
1 celery stalk, cut into coarse pieces
2 cloves of garlic

Directions

Pour all the water into a large pot, add the bones and kombu seaweed. Stir well and let stand 5 minutes. Add the onion, celery, and peeled garlic. Stir again.

Raise the heat and let the broth simmer for at least 4 hours, until the bones are well cooked and the broth has a milky white color; it may take 1 to 2 hours longer depending on the pot you use or the size of the piece of bone.

Remove the bones and other ingredients from the broth with a skimmer. Let the broth cool and then store it in the refrigerator.

The next day, remove the foam and solidified fat on the surface. Bring the broth to a simmer and use it to make your ramen.

Shio

Shio is the older version and therefore perhaps closer to what was eaten in the 1950s, the broth is made with chicken or fish, and vegetables. There is no perfect dosage of these elements, the important thing is that you can taste all the flavors.

The broth of shio ramen is clear, tending to yellow and rather salty (shio, in fact, means "salt"). Some people also add pork bones, typical of Tonkotsu, but they are not boiled for long so the broth remains pale and light. I personally do not use them, preferring to keep a lighter flavor.

Here's how to make shio broth for ramen:

Ingredients

7 liters of water
2 kg of chicken bones or 1.5 kg of fish
100 g of kombu seaweed
50 g sea salt

1 medium onion, cut in half
2 cloves of garlic, crushed
2 carrots, cut into coarse pieces
1 celery stalk, cut into coarse pieces

Directions

Put the water in a large pot, add the chicken bones or fish, kombu seaweed and salt. Turn on the heat and let it cook for about 15 minutes. Add the onion, garlic, carrots, and celery. Stir again.

Lower the heat and let the broth simmer for at least 3 hours, until the bones are well cooked and the broth has a nice golden color.

If you prepare it the day before, remove the bones and other ingredients from the broth, let it cool and refrigerate. The next day, remove the foam on the surface, bring the broth to a simmer and use it to make your ramen.

Shoyu

With a strong soy sauce flavor, this broth is light brown in color, usually made from chicken and vegetables, (you can also use fish or beef) and a generous addition of soy sauce, the result is an intense, salty but still fairly light flavor that is not overly fatty.

Here is how to make shoyu broth:

Ingredients

7 liters of water
1 kg of chicken bones or 1 kg of fish
100 g of kombu seaweed
70 ml soy sauce

1 medium onion, cut in half
2 cloves of garlic, crushed
2 carrots, cut into coarse pieces
1 celery stalk, cut into coarse pieces

Directions

Put the water in a large pot, add the bones, kombu seaweed, onion, garlic, carrots and celery. Stir well and turn on the heat to a very low flame.

Let the broth simmer for at least 4 hours, stirring occasionally until the bones are well cooked and the broth has a nice golden color.

If you prepare it the day before, remove the bones and other ingredients from the broth, let it cool, and then refrigerate it. The next day, remove the foam and solidified fat on the surface. Bring the broth to a boil and add the soy sauce. Stir well and use the broth to make your ramen.

Miso

It is the newest of the four and is a purely Japanese recipe; it has no Chinese origins. It was first produced in Hokkaido in 1965 and features a broth that combines the classic chicken or fish broth with a large amount of miso.

To make miso broth for ramen, you can follow this recipe:

Ingredients

7 liters of water
1 kg of chicken bones or 1 kg of fish
100 g of kombu seaweed
60 g miso paste

1 medium onion, cut in half
2 cloves of garlic, crushed
2 carrots, cut into coarse pieces
1 celery stalk, cut into coarse pieces

Directions

Put the water in a large pot, add the bones, kombu seaweed, onion, garlic, carrots and celery. Stir well and turn the heat on low.

Let the broth simmer for at least 3 hours, until the bones are well cooked and the broth has a nice golden color.

If you prepare it the day before, remove the bones and other ingredients from the broth, let it cool and then refrigerate it. The next day, remove the foam and solidified fat on the surface, bring the broth to a boil and add the miso paste. Stir well and use the broth to make your ramen.

Easier Broths

Let us now look at three other broths that are less traditional and simpler to prepare. The minimum cooking time is always at least 1 1/2 hours, but other than that they are not complex. Consider them quicker "basics" that you can use to create your dishes.

With the exception of vegetable broth, they are basically composed of a protein and a mix of vegetables, so they do not have that aromatic base typical of more traditional broths. This is not a problem; on the contrary, precisely because they are more neutral, they can be used in a wide range of recipes, and the end result will still be tasty.

Vegetable Broth

Vegetable broth is the basic preparation for almost every vegetarian and vegan dish in this book. The absence of animal parts and the rich taste given by vegetables make it perfect for use in complex, spicy recipes. To make vegetable broth these are the ingredients you will need.

Ingredients

7 liters of water
2 carrots
2 onions
1 medium potato
1 celery stalk
1 tomato

150 g cauliflower, if you do not have cauliflower you can use broccoli or squash
1 pinch of salt.
1 tablespoon of olive oil or seed oil
3-4 whole black peppercorns
Aromatic herbs to taste (parsley, thyme, marjoram, etc.)

Directions

Cut all the vegetables into small pieces and put them in a pot. Add water, enough to cover them completely; I recommend using at least 7 liters. Turn the heat on low and let it cook for about 45 minutes, stirring occasionally.

After this time has elapsed, add the herbs, salt and pepper. Continue cooking for another 45 minutes. Remove the vegetables from the broth and strain it, to make it smoother. Add the oil, this will give more roundness to the flavor given by the vegetables.

You can use it right away or store it in the refrigerator for 2-3 days. In case you decide to use it later you can also freeze it.

Meat Broth

To make meat stock you will need:

Ingredients

14 liters of water

1 kg beef or chicken bones

2 onions

2 carrots

1 celery stalk

2 cloves of garlic

3-4 whole black peppercorns

Aromatic herbs to taste (parsley, thyme, marjoram, etc.)

Directions

Put the bones in a large pot and cover with half the water. Bring to a boil and let simmer for 5 minutes. Drain the water and rinse the bones under cold water to remove impurities and foam.

Put the bones back in the pot and add the chopped vegetables, herbs, and a little salt. Cover with cold water (at least 7 liters), turn on the heat to medium and bring to a boil.

Lower the heat and let the broth simmer for at least an hour and a half; if you have time, you can let it simmer even longer. Strain the broth through a strainer to remove all impurities.

The meat stock is ready, You can use it right away or store it in the refrigerator for 2-3 days. In case you decide to use it later you can also freeze it.

Fish Broth

To make fish stock you will need:

Ingredients

7 liters of water

1 kg heads, bones or carapaces

1 onion

1 carrot

1 celery stalk

2 cloves of garlic

3-4 whole black peppercorns

1 tomato

Aromatic herbs to taste (parsley, thyme, marjoram, etc.)

Directions

Put the fish heads and bones in a large pot and turn on the heat. Let them cook for 5 minutes and mash them with a spoon to release all the fish flavor. Add the water and cook for another 5 minutes.

Add the chopped vegetables, herbs, a little salt and pepper. Lower the heat and let the broth simmer for about 1 hour and 30 minutes. Strain the broth through a strainer, removing the heads and bones and vegetables.

After this time has elapsed, the fish stock will be ready. You can use it right away or store it in the refrigerator for 2-3 days. In case you decide to use it later you can also freeze it.

The element that makes the difference: the Noodle Ramen

There is no ramen without good noodles! But what exactly are they?

Noodles are one of the most widely consumed foods in Asian countries, not only in Japan. There are, in fact, endless versions of them, they can be made with wheat flour, rice flour, potato flour, they can be with or without eggs, they can be fresh or dried, in short, there is no limit to the imagination.

Let's be clear about the Name...

Before continuing, to avoid misunderstandings, it is good to clarify the correct name of this type of noodle. The term "Noodle" generally means any long noodle; as you will see shortly, there are several types.

Among the many types of long noodles, there is one in particular that is best suited for use in ramen because of its texture. This type is called "Noodle Ramen" or even simply "Ramen." By the term Ramen then, it is possible to mean either the noodle type or the whole dish (complete with broth, vegetables, and everything else); as you can imagine some times, there is confusion.

In this book, for the sake of clarity, I will try to always use the full name "Noodle Ramen," meaning the type of noodle most suitable for use in ramen.

The Secret to Making Great Noodle Ramen

The main characteristic of this type of noodle is the texture, which is more elastic than normal, making them perfect for eating together with hot broth.

To make excellent ramen noodles you need a real...secret ingredient!

To make any kind of fresh noodle no doubt you have to use quality flours, but in this case it is not enough. To make excellent ramen noodles, one must necessarily use an alkaline base. Alkalinity is the secret that makes these noodles special.

It will, in fact, not only give the noodles the right consistency to be eaten with hot broth, but it will also give them that yellowish color typical of ramen noodles. To achieve the right alkalinity, simply use kansui.

To make excellent noodle ramen the list of ingredients is very short, but it is essential to stick to it fully, you need, in fact, only good flour, water, kansui and a pinch of salt.

Are you ready to knead?

Kansui

Kansui is that secret ingredient that gives the right texture (and also the right flavor) to ramen noodles. It's not a hard ingredient to find, but you can't find it everywhere either!

So you're telling me that I have to go around to all the stores in my town looking for kansui?

But no, rest assured, it is also possible to make it at home with a very simple process. I'll explain how.

The only ingredient you'll need is baking soda (sodium or potassium); we'll use it as a base to make kansui.

It weighs about 100 g of baking soda. Turn on the oven to 120 °C, take a baking sheet, cover it with foil and lay the baking soda on top. Leave it in the oven for about 1 hour; this will increase the baking soda's pH, becoming even more alkaline, and it will lose about 1/3 of its weight.

After this time has passed, remove it from the oven and weigh it on a scale, if the weight is between 60 and 70 g then the kansui will be ready, otherwise put it back in the oven for a few minutes.

As you can see it is a very simple process, with this small amount you can knead enough dough to create 44 servings of ramen!

The Recipe for Perfect Ramen Noodles

Here are the ingredients needed for 4 people:

Ingredients

200 g of 0 flour   *6 g kansui*
200 g 00 flour   *1 pinch of salt*
160 ml water

Directions

Combine the salt with the flours and sift them twice, this step is to prevent lumps from forming. In a separate bowl mix the water with the kansui.

Add the liquid ingredients to the dry ingredients a little at a time and knead directly with your hands until you get a compact mass.

Once all the flour has been added, knead it 5 minutes with your hands, after which place it in a bowl, cover with plastic wrap and let it rest at room temperature for 1 hour.

Once it has rested, dust the table with a fistful of flour, take about 1/3 of the dough and roll it out to a sheet with an even thickness of about 2 millimeters. You can use a rolling pin or, if you have one, a pasta machine.

Do not use too much flour to dust the dough as you work it, because there is already a lot of flour; adding more dry part would make the dough too hard and no longer workable.

The first time you make the dough roll it out to the thickness I suggested, because that way it will be very easy to cut, later you can increase or decrease it slightly according to your taste. If you own a pasta machine, also use it to cut the noodles precisely.

If, on the other hand, you don't have one, you will have to do it by hand, no problem, you just need a little extra manual dexterity. To cut the dough by hand once you have rolled it out, helping yourself with a cutting board, cut the noodles, about 3 mm thick. This is the cleanest method, but also the one that requires the most dexterity and precision. Alternatively, sprinkle a minimum of flour (mind you, very little) on the sheet, roll it up to form a roll and cut it into slices, also 3 mm thick.

Repeat the process for the entire dough and you will have created fantastic and delicious homemade ramen noodles!

How to store dough properly

Handmade dough can be stored for a long time by following a few simple steps.

After making the dough, let it dry for an hour or two on a floured work surface or on a tablecloth. Make sure the noodles are spaced well apart to prevent sticking.

Once dry, cover it with plastic wrap or wrap it in a plastic bag. Be sure to remove as much air as possible before closing the bag. You can store it in the refrigerator for up to 15 days.

If you want to store the dough for a longer period, you can freeze it. To do this, place the noodles wrapped in plastic wrap or plastic bag in an airtight container or freezer food bag. In the freezer, noodles can be stored for up to 6 months.

"I don't have time to make fresh pasta, how can I do it?"

I'm sure you've thought that at least once!

Don't worry, I fully understand that you don't work in a restaurant, and that you may not have time (or don't feel like it, no harm in that) to make fresh pasta every time as well. Does this mean you have to give up enjoying a good ramen? Absolutely not! I propose three simple and effective solutions:

- *Use commercial dry pasta.* That's right, you got it right, you can also use plain packaged spaghetti, which can be bought in any supermarket. If you use this, however, you will have to be careful when cooking to add a generous tablespoon of baking soda. This will introduce the alkalinity needed to make them more elastic and more like ramen noodles made with kansui. Remember that the cooking time in this case increases, generally it should be boiled for 6-8 minutes, but always check the directions on the package.
- *Buy ready-made ramen noodles.* You can find them in most well-stocked supermarkets or specialty stores, they are not easy to find, but not difficult either, nowadays you can find any kind of product.
- *Make them yourself and freeze them.* This is a compromise it is true, but think about it for a second, by being able to freeze them you can make ramen noodles once and eat them on several occasions. I assure you that among the three proposed solutions this will be the one you will adopt most often, and after making them a couple of times, you will get the hang of it and the whole process will be fast and fun.

There is no such thing as just Ramen! Other Types of Oriental Noodles

The most versatile - Soba

Soba is a Japanese noodle made from buckwheat flour, which is used to make noodles. Soba noodles are usually served in a bowl with a hot broth, to which ingredients such as tofu, vegetables and meat are added. They can also be served in salads or stir-fried. Soba is very popular in Japan and is often eaten during the summertime, as it is believed to help combat the heat.

Thin Noodles - Shirataki

Shirataki are a type of Japanese noodle made from konjac, a plant native to Asia. They are very thin and have a gelatinous texture. They are often used as a substitute for noodles in many dishes, such as ramen, because they have very few calories and carbohydrates. Shirataki noodles are usually sold canned and must be rinsed before use. They can be eaten hot or cold and go very well with soy sauces, vegetables, and meat.

On Hot Summer Days - Hiyamugi

Hiyamugi is a type of noodle made from wheat flour, water and salt. It is usually served cold, accompanied by a light soy sauce. Hiyamugi noodles are often topped with vegetables and tofu, but can also be served with other ingredients such as meat or fish. In Japan, hiyamugi is often eaten during the summertime, as it is believed to help combat the heat. It has a soft texture and mild flavor, making it popular outside the country as well.

Most Popular - Udon

Udon are a type of Japanese noodles made from wheat flour, water and salt. They are very thick and have a round shape, similar to that of noodles. They are usually served in a bowl with a hot broth, to which ingredients such as tofu, vegetables and meat are added, but they can also be served in a salad or stir-fried. Udon are very popular in Japan and have become a popular dish in other countries as well. They are easy to prepare and can be enjoyed both hot and cold.

Make your own Ramen using Typical Ingredients from Japanese Culture.

In this chapter I will briefly introduce you to some of the most typical ingredients of Japanese cuisine. You won't find all of them in the recipes in this book, but I think it is important to know them, because that way you can customize ramen as you see fit, being sure to retain that oriental flavor characteristic of Japanese cuisine.

The Cinderella of Cooking, Negi

The negi is a type of onion typical of Japanese cuisine. It is usually longer and thinner than a regular onion and has a slightly sweeter and less pungent flavor. It is often used as a condiment for ramen, as an ingredient for takoyaki (an octopus specialty), or as a garnish for other Japanese cuisine dishes. In addition, negi is often used as an ingredient for making sauces to season dishes. It can be cut into thin slices and used as a garnish for sushi or other fish or meat preparations. In addition, negi can be used as a seasoning for soups and stews.

Eggs? No, better! Ajitsuke tamago

Ajitsuke tamago are eggs marinated in soy sauce. They are hard-boiled eggs that are soaked in a solution of soy sauce, ginger, and sake until they take on a dark color and intense flavor. Once ready, ajitsuke tamago are usually cut in half and served as a side dish for ramen, rice, or as a snack. They have a slightly sweet and slightly salty taste, and are highly valued for their intense and distinctive flavor.

The Taste of Eastern Forests, Menma

Menma is a common ingredient in Japanese cuisine; it is a type of marinated and cooked bamboo. It is prepared from bamboo, marinated in a mixture of soy sauce, sake, sugar and spices. After being marinated for some time, menma is cooked in a pan or steamed until tender. It is often used as a condiment for ramen, but can also be served as a side dish or as an ingredient in other recipes.

Long-cooked meat, chashu

Chasu is a type of barbecued pork that originated in Japanese cuisine. Pork is thinly sliced and marinated in a mixture of soy sauce, sake and spices. After being marinated, the meat is cooked for many hours on the grill or barbecued until tender. Chasu is often used as a condiment for ramen or as an ingredient in other Japanese cuisine recipes.

A Root with a Thousand Properties, Ginger

Ginger is an aromatic root used as a spice in many Asian cuisine dishes, both sweet and savory. It is native to tropical Asia, but is also cultivated in many other countries around the world. Ginger has a spicy and slightly sweet taste, and is often used to add flavor to meat, fish, vegetable or sweet dishes. It is also often used in herbal medicine for its digestive and refreshing properties. Ginger can be eaten fresh or dried, grated or powdered, and is also often used to make herbal teas or refreshing drinks.

What about marinating it? Here's the gari

Gari is a type of marinated ginger that originated in Japanese cuisine. It is prepared with slices of fresh ginger marinated in a solution of soy sauce, sugar and rice vinegar. It is left to marinate for several hours or even days until it becomes soft and its flavor becomes slightly sweet and sour. Gari is often served as a side dish with sushi or other Japanese cuisine, but it can also be used as a condiment for other recipes.

The Base for Sauces You Don't Expect, Katsoubushi

Katsuobushi is an ingredient in Japanese cuisine made from dried and smoked tuna. It is made from tuna steaks, which are air-dried for several months and then smoked with beech wood. Once dried and smoked, the tuna steaks are ground to a fine powder. Katsuobushi is used as a seasoning for dashi, a basic broth used as a base for many dishes in Japanese cuisine, and is also used to flavor other recipes, such as ramen.

The Flavor of the Earth, Daikon

Daikon is a type of white turnip that is very common in Asian cuisine. It has a cylindrical shape and a thin, delicate skin. It has a slightly sweet and pungent flavor and is used in many Japanese, Chinese, and Korean cuisine dishes. It is often grated and used as a topping or garnish for sushi, it is thinly sliced and used as an ingredient for takoyaki, or it is diced and used as a topping for ramen.

Tofu, Much More Than a Vegan Food

Tofu, also called "soy cheese," is a soy-based food that is popular in Asia and now in other parts of the world. It is made from ground soybeans, which are cooked and then pressed to extract the milk. The soy milk is then coagulated, using a coagulating agent such as calcium chloride or citric acid, and then pressed to remove excess water. Tofu has a texture similar to cream cheese and can be used in many ways in cooking, both as an ingredient in savory and sweet dishes. It is highly valued for its versatility and high protein and other nutrient content.

The Taste of the Sea, Kombu Seaweed

Kombu is a type of brown seaweed native to Japan. It is often used as an ingredient to make dashi, a broth used as a base for many Japanese dishes. Kombu is also used to marinate meat or fish, to flavor soups and stews, or to add flavor to other recipes. It is rich in nutrients and is often regarded as a medicinal food in Japan.

Nori Seaweed Sheets

Nori seaweed is a type of dried seaweed native to Japan. It is sold in thin sheets, has a dark green color, and is mainly used to wrap sushi, or in ramen dishes. It is also valued for its medicinal properties and is often used in traditional Japanese preparations to treat various diseases.

How Much Sea in Japan Wakame Seaweed

Wakame is a type of seaweed, native to Japan. It has a dark green color and a soft, juicy texture. It is used in many Japanese cuisine dishes, such as miso shiru (miso soup), sunomono (marinated vegetable salad), and wakame salad (wakame salad). In addition, wakame is often used to enrich soups and broths with other types of seaweed.

Not just Manga, Narutomaki

Narutomaki is an ingredient in Japanese cuisine made from dried and smoked fish, usually tuna, which is ground to a powder. It is then mixed with wheat flour and other ingredients to form a dough, which is cut into thin slices and cooked in a pan. Narutomaki is round in shape and has a spiral pattern on the surface, which gives it the name "narutomaki" (naruto means "swirl" in Japanese). It is often used as a topping for ramen or as a garnish for other Japanese dishes.

Typically Oriental Flavors: Fermented Foods, Sauces and Beverages

Miso

Miso is a Japanese fermented paste made from soybeans, barley or rice. It is made by mixing soybeans with a mushroom called koji and a small amount of salt. The mixture is then left to mature for several months or years, until it becomes a thick, flavorful paste. Miso is used in many Japanese dishes, such as ramen or miso soup, and is also often used as a dressing for salads, vegetables, and meat. It has a slightly salty and umami flavor.

Miso Tare

Miso tare is a concentrated miso sauce used in many Japanese dishes, such as ramen or yakiniku. It is made by boiling miso along with other ingredients such as sake, mirin, and sugar to a thick, flavorful consistency. It is used to flavor broth or to marinate meat or fish before being cooked. Miso tare has an intense umami flavor, and is often used as a base for many other Japanese condiments and sauces.

Shio Tare

Shio tare is a light soy sauce used in many Japanese dishes, such as ramen or yakiniku. It is made by boiling soy sauce together with other ingredients such as sake, mirin, and sugar until a thick, flavorful consistency is achieved. It is used to flavor broth or to marinate meat or fish before being cooked. Shio tare has a light, salty flavor, and is often used as a base for many other Japanese condiments and sauces. The term "shio" means "salt" in Japanese, while "tare" means "sauce."

Teriyaki sauce

Teriyaki sauce is a giappones sauce, which is used to marinate or season meat or fish before it is cooked. Teriyaki sauce has a sweet and slightly spicy flavor, and is often used to prepare teriyaki chicken or tuna, which are cooked on the grill or in a pan. Teriyaki sauce is usually prepared by boiling all the ingredients together until the liquid thickens and becomes thick. It is often served hot, but can also be used as a dressing for salads or other cold dishes.

Furikake

Furikake is a Japanese condiment made from seeds, seaweed, and spices that is used to flavor rice dishes. Furikake is usually drizzled over hot rice or used as a dressing for rice salads. There are many types of furikake, each with a different mixture of ingredients, but they usually contain toasted sesame seeds, dried seaweed, and spices such as cucumber or onion. Furikake has a slightly salty, umami flavor, and is often used to add a touch of flavor in otherwise simple dishes.

Gomasium

Gomasio is a Japanese seasoning made from toasted sesame seeds and sea salt, which is used to flavor rice dishes. Gomasio is usually sprinkled over hot rice or used as a dressing for rice salads. It has a slightly salty and slightly sweet taste, and is often used to add a touch of flavor in otherwise simple dishes. Gomasio is prepared by grinding toasted sesame seeds with a mortar or food processor, then mixing them with sea salt to a powdery consistency. It is a popular seasoning in Japan and is often used in macrobiotic cooking.

Nikumiso

Nikumiso is a Japanese sauce made from ground pork, miso and sake, which is used to season or marinate meat or rice. It has a slightly salty taste and is often used to prepare nikujaga, which is a dish of pork and vegetables cooked in a dashi broth. Nikumiso is usually prepared by boiling all the ingredients together until the liquid thickens and becomes thick. It is often served hot, but can also be used as a dressing for salads or other cold dishes.

Sakè

Sake is a Japanese alcoholic beverage made by fermenting rice. It is made by cooking rice and adding a fungus called koji, which converts starches into sugar. The mixture is then left to ferment for several months, until it becomes an alcoholic beverage with a mild, slightly sweet taste. Sake is usually served in small ceramic cups and is often consumed during meals or ceremonies. It has an alcohol content of between 14 percent and 20 percent.

Mirin

Mirin is an alcoholic liquid with an alcohol content of about 14 percent and a fairly high sugar content. The production technique resembles that of sake, but the final product is very different. It is produced by cooking rice, then adding koji. The mixture is then left to ferment for several months, until it becomes takes on a sweet, slightly caramelized taste. Mirin is usually used in cooking as a seasoning, to flavor dishes or to make teriyaki sauce.

Recipes of My Life

Tips for use

We have now come to the "heart" of the book, the actual recipes. In the making of ramen there are many processes that take time, such as preparing the broth. My advice is (if you have the chance) to get ahead and prepare them perhaps the day before.

Ramen has four classic broths, as I explained earlier, but in many recipes I have preferred to make small variations, both to vary the flavors from time to time and to show you that this dish is not a science, nor a chemical formula. In the list of ingredients some times you will find the actual broth (e.g. Tonkotsu, Miso, vegetable...the recipes are in the appropriate chapter), others you will find the ingredients and the process to make it. Remember that by cooking you can create and express yourself.

If you want to customize my recipes even more, but at the same time you want to be sure not to lose that "oriental" taste, I suggest you use the ingredients described in the previous chapter, typical of Japanese culture and cuisine. Create new combinations, substitute one ingredient for another, change the garnish of a dish, in other words...have fun! Experiment as much as you can and customize my recipes as you see fit to create YOUR ramen.

Maybe one day I will be the one to read your cookbook, I would love to!

Meat Ramen

Ramen with Pork Loin and Bamboo Slices

Servings: 4   **Preparation Time: 90 minutes**

600 g ramen noodles

2 eggs

2 tablespoons toasted sesame seeds

For the broth

5 liters of water

2 tablespoons seed oil

1 pork loin of at least 600 g

3 spring onions

5 slices of ginger

3 tablespoons of soy sauce

3 tablespoons of sake

1 tablespoon sugar

100 g bamboo slices

Directions

First thing you need to prepare the broth. To do this, heat the seed oil in a pot and start browning the pork loin, making sure to turn it every 3 minutes so that it is evenly cooked. After browning it on all sides, add the coarsely chopped spring onions, sliced ginger, soy sauce, bamboo slices, sake and sugar and fill with water until the meat is covered. Now cook the whole thing over medium heat for about 90 minutes.

After this time remove the meat from the broth, cut it into slices and set aside.

Bring a pot of water to a boil, cook the eggs inside for 5 minutes, remove them, let them cool and remove the shell.

In another saucepan, bring water to a boil and cook the noodles for 3 minutes or according to the directions on the package. When ready, remove them from the water and set aside.

Divide the noodles into bowls, pour the broth over them until they are covered, and top the dish with the slices of meat and eggs cut in half. Garnish with a handful of toasted sesame seeds.

Shoyu Ramen with Pork Belly

Servings: 2 **Preparation Time: 1 hour and 15 minutes**

300 g ramen noodles *1 egg* *4 tablespoons soy sauce*
600 ml of shoyu broth *4 dried shiitake* *40 g fresh arugula*
1 piece of pork belly of at *mushrooms* *2 sheets of nori seaweed*
least 250 g *1 tablespoon paprika* *A few sprigs of chives*

Directions

The first thing to do is to boil the pork belly 10 minutes in water, to which you will have added ginger slices, so as to remove excess fat. Having done this brief step, remove it from the water, season it with paprika and soy sauce and bake it in the oven at 220° for about 1 hour. After this time has elapsed, turn off the oven, but leave the meat inside so that it does not experience abrupt changes in temperature.

Heat the broth, cut the mushrooms into long slices and pour them inside, taking care to cook them for at least 15 minutes.

In a saucepan, bring water to a boil and cook the egg for about 5 minutes. When it is ready, remove it from the water, let it cool and peel it.

In another pot, bring water to a boil and cook the noodles for 3 minutes or according to package directions. When ready drain them and divide them into bowls.

Divide noodles into bowls and pour hot broth with mushrooms until covered. Lay the sliced pork belly on top and garnish with the arugula, nori seaweed and chopped chives.

Miso Ramen with Sweet and Sour Duck Legs

Servings: 2   **Preparation Time: 2 hours**

300 g ramen noodles

600 ml Miso broth

2 Duck Legs

3 slices of fresh ginger

6 tablespoons honey

2 eggs

60 g asparagus

1 tablespoon seed or olive oil

100 g fresh chiodini mushrooms

1 spring onion

1 fresh chili pepper

25 g soybean sprouts

1 tablespoon of sesame seeds

Directions

Start the preparation of this dish by processing the duck legs. The first thing to do is to boil them 5 minutes in water, to which you will have added slices of ginger, so as to remove excess fat. Having done this brief step, spread the honey over the meat and bake it in the oven at 220° for about 1 hour and 30 minutes (even 2 hours if the piece is particularly large). After this time has elapsed turn off the oven, but leave the meat inside so that it does not undergo abrupt changes in temperature.

In a small saucepan bring water to a boil and cook the eggs for about 5 minutes. When they are ready, remove them from the water, let them cool and peel them.

Heat a tablespoon of oil in a skillet; when hot, lay the asparagus inside and cook for 5 minutes, turning them so they are evenly cooked.

In a saucepan bring the broth to a boil and cook the noodles inside for 3 minutes or according to package directions. When ready drain them and divide them into bowls.

Complete the dish by filling the bowls with the broth, lay the duck thighs, asparagus, eggs, and chiodini mushrooms on top. Garnish with the soybean sprouts, sesame seeds, spring onion and sliced chili.

"Hungarian" Ramen

Servings: 2

Preparation Time: 2 hours and 30 minutes

300 g ramen noodles
2 dried shiitake mushrooms
1 egg
100 g broccoli
1 sheet of nori seaweed
2 tablespoons of soy sauce

1 teaspoon of tomato paste
1 star anise
½ teaspoon pepper
1 tablespoon olive oil
½ teaspoon fresh coriander
For the broth

150 g celery
150 g carrot
150 g leek
3 cloves of garlic
150 g onion
2 over chicken thighs

Directions

Start the recipe with the two most time-consuming preparations of all: the broth and the mushrooms. To prepare the broth, soak the chicken overthighs in a large pot filled with cold water along with garlic, leek, onion, celery and carrots, all roughly chopped except for the carrots. Turn the heat on low and let it cook for about two hours.

Soak the mushrooms in warm water; they will need about 30 minutes to be ready.

While you are waiting for the broth and mushrooms to be ready take all the spices and chop them finely. Ideally you should use a mortar, this way you will fully preserve all their aroma, alternatively an electric mixer is fine too. Once you have minced the spices, set them aside in a small dish.

After about two hours the broth should be ready, and you will need to reduce it to intensify the flavor. To do this, remove the chicken and all the vegetables from inside and set them aside. Add the ginger slices, mushrooms, spices and tomato paste. Turn up the heat and continue cooking for 30 minutes.

Separately, cook the eggs. Take a small saucepan and bring it to a boil. When the water boils gently dip the egg with the whole shell and hold it exactly 5 minutes. This way you will have an egg with the white cooked and the yolk soft. Of course it is a matter of taste, if you like it more cooked, let it boil a few minutes longer.

Wash the broccoli thoroughly under running water, cut it into pieces and then very simply cook it in a pan for 5 minutes together with a tablespoon of oil. When it is ready, take the chicken you have set aside and add it to the pan over high heat for 2 minutes, just long enough for it to flavor a little.

When the broth is almost ready, bring another pot to a boil to cook the pasta. Once the water is boiling, soak the ramen noodles for about 3 minutes. If you are using the dry ones, leave them for twice as long.

When this last ingredient is also ready, you can assemble the dish. Take a nice large bowl and fill it halfway with the broth. Dip the noodles inside and later all the ingredients, including the nori seaweed sheets and a tablespoon of soy sauce.

Ramen with Spiced Pork Belly

Servings: 4   **Preparation Time: 3 hours**

600 g ramen noodles   *4 tablespoons of soy*   *30 g Miso paste*
2000 ml Tonkotsu broth   *sauce*   *80 g Spring onion*
300 g Pork Belly   *4 eggs*   *80 g Carrots*
4 cloves of fresh garlic   *4 tablespoons soy sauce*   *2 Sheets of nori seaweed*
2 inches of ginger   *for the eggs*   *80 g Leek*
1 chili pepper   *10 ml Mirin*   *2 tablespoons chopped*
100 ml sake   *1 pinch of black pepper*   *cilantro*

Directions

hot a frying pan, when it is well heated, brown the pork belly inside on all sides, starting with the skin side, which takes the longest.

Toward the end of the cooking time, add the garlic, chili and ginger. Add the sake, mirin and half the soy sauce. Sauté a few minutes, after which place in a baking dish, with a lid, and place in the oven. Bake at 160° for two and a half hours, making sure to turn the meat every 40 minutes. If you see that it becomes too dry, add a ladleful of broth.

Separately in a small saucepan bring about 1 liter of water to a boil and pour the eggs inside. Let them cook for 5 minutes, remove the shells and marinate them in the soy sauce.

Heat the broth, add the miso, soy sauce and spices. Cut the vegetables into julienne strips and season them with the rest of the soy sauce.

Cook the noodles separately in a pot of boiling water for about 3 minutes if you are using fresh noodles, 6 minutes otherwise.

Divide the noodles among four bowls. Add 2 ladles of hot strained broth, the eggs and nori seaweed cut in half, and finish with the cilantro and pork belly.

Tonkotsu Ramen with Pork Shoulder

Servings: 2 **Preparation Time: 4 hours**

300 g ramen noodles
1 piece of pork shoulder of at least 350 g
3 tablespoons of soy sauce
2 tablespoons rice vinegar

1 shallot
2 cloves of garlic
1 spring onion
1 tablespoon black peppercorns
600 ml Tonkotsu broth
1 egg

1 red onion
A few sprigs of chives
1 fresh chili pepper

Directions

In a bowl let the pork shoulder marinate one hour with soy sauce, rice vinegar, shallots, garlic, spring onion, and peppercorns.

Turn on the oven to 200° C and cook the meat, with all the liquids from the marinade, for at least 3 hours. The cooking time depends greatly on the size of the piece, and can also vary greatly. To make sure it is well cooked, take it out of the oven, let it cool 5 minutes and try fraying it with your hands, if the meat breaks easily, then it is cooked, otherwise put it back in the oven.

When the meat is almost ready, start heating the broth.

Boil the egg for about 8 minutes, well cooked eggs go better in this dish. When it is ready, remove it from the water, let it cool and peel it.

In a saucepan, bring water to a boil and cook the noodles for 3 minutes or according to package directions. When ready drain them and divide them into bowls.

Fill the bowls with the broth, add a portion of pork shoulder and the egg cut in half. Top the dish with finely chopped red onion, chopped chives, and sliced fresh chili.

Simple Chicken Ramen

Servings: 2   **Preparation Time: 1 hour and 15 minutes**

300 g ramen noodles   *2 eggs*   *1 branch of parsley*
3 slices of fresh ginger   *1 spring onion*   *1 carrot*
1 clove of garlic   ***For the broth***   *1 bay leaf*
1 tablespoon sesame oil   *800 g chicken pieces*   *4 black peppercorns*
3 tablespoons soy sauce   *1 spring onion*

Directions

Put the chicken in a pot with a spring onion, carrot, parsley, bay leaf and pepper. Cover with water, bring to a boil and cook for about 1 hour. Meanwhile, finely chop the other spring onion, ginger and garlic and brown them in a pan with a tablespoon of sesame oil over medium heat. When browned in the oil, add plenty of soy sauce.

Remove the chicken from the pan, cut it into small pieces, and cook it in the pan with the vegetables for 10 minutes. Strain the broth through a colander and return it to the pan without the vegetables.

Boil water in a saucepan, add the eggs and cook for about 5 minutes. Remove them from the water, let them cool and cut them in half.

Pour a quarter of the broth into the pot with the spices and chicken, mix well with a spatula and use it as a seasoning. Cook the noodles in the remaining broth and serve with the chicken and sliced spring onion.

Ramen with Duck and Spicy Seaweed

Servings: 4   **Preparation Time: 3 hours**

600 g ramen noodles	*2 tablespoons soy sauce*	***For the broth***
12 skiitake mushrooms	*2 sheets of nori seaweed*	*1 duck*
4 tablespoons seed or olive oil	*2 tablespoons miso*	*1 celery stalk*
1 clove of garlic	*2 fresh chilies*	*2 carrots*
		1 spring onion
		3 liters of water

Directions

Remove the duck breast and save it for later use. Remove the thighs; peel the celery, carrot and spring onion. Chop the vegetables and add them, along with the thighs and other bones, to a pot of about 5 liters of cold water. Bring to a boil, then simmer for 3 hours. Remove the foam from time to time with a spoon.

Soak the skiitake mushrooms in warm water for about 1 hour, after which cut them into slices and saute them in a pan with a tablespoon of oil for a few minutes. Set them aside; we will use them for the garnish.

Meanwhile, peel the garlic and brown it lightly in a pan with a tablespoon of oil. Add the soy sauce and dissolve the miso paste in it. Pour the mixture into bowls.

Cook the noodles in boiling water for 3 minutes or as long as indicated on the package.

Cut the chili and nori seaweed into thin strips.

Fry the duck fillets skin-side down in a pan with the remaining oil for 5 minutes until crispy. Then turn them over and cook for another 2 minutes. Let the breasts rest for a while, cut them into slices about 1 cm thick and add them to the miso mixture in bowls. Add the noodles, thigh meat and mushrooms. Pour over the hot soup, lay the rest of the ingredients on top, and serve.

Tonkotsu Ramen with Marinated Bacon

Servings: 2   **Preparation Time: 2 hours**

300 g ramen noodles   *1 tablespoon of soy sauce*   *1 tablespoon of rice*
600 ml Tonkotsu broth   *3 slices of fresh ginger*   *vinegar*
250 g pork belly   *2 tablespoons honey*   *2 tablespoons olive or*
1 egg   *1 clove of garlic*   *seed oil*
1 sprig of chives   *1 shallot*   *1 carrot*
10 chard leaves

Directions

In a large bowl, pour the pork belly and add the soy sauce, fresh ginger, minced garlic clove, honey, minced shallots, and rice vinegar. Let it marinate for about an hour.

After this time has elapsed, light a frying pan and, when it is hot, lay the bacon inside on the skin side. It is important that the heat is not excessive, otherwise you will not be able to cook the fat properly. Let it go for about 10 minutes, turn it over and cook for another 10 minutes. Now complete cooking in the oven at 180°C for 20 minutes. Remove from the oven and let rest. If you don't like having "long" sliced bacon in the dish, you can roll it up, secure it with a toothpick or piece of string, and then slice it.

Boil the egg for about 5 minutes, this way you will have the egg white well cooked and the yolk soft. When it is ready, remove it from the water, let it cool and peel it.

In a saucepan, bring water to a boil and cook the noodles for 3 minutes or according to the directions on the package. When ready, remove them from the water and set aside. Heat the broth.

Pour 2 tablespoons of oil into a skillet; when hot, cook the chard until wilted; this will take about 5 minutes. Wash the carrot and cut it into sticks.

Divide the noodles into bowls, pour the broth over them, and top the dish with bacon slices, halved eggs, carrot sticks, chard, and chopped chives.

Shoyu Ramen with Fried Chicken

Servings: 2   **Preparation Time: 35 minutes**

300 g ramen noodles	*2 tablespoons miso paste*	*About 150 g panko*
1000 ml of shoyu broth	*150 g of 00 flour*	*1000 ml seed oil*
20 g fresh ginger	*1 tablespoon paprika*	*2 eggs*
100 ml sake	*1 clove of garlic*	*4 tablespoons of soy sauce*
2 tablespoons mirin	*1 tablespoon chili powder*	

Directions

First, boil the broth over high heat in one pot. In a second pot cut ginger into very small pieces, add sake, mirin and miso paste, cook for about 10 minutes stirring constantly. Once ready set aside and pass through a sieve to make it finer.

In a bowl, mix flour with paprika powder, minced garlic and chili powder. In another bowl, crack and beat an egg. In the last bowl, pour panko.

Dip the chicken in the flour with the flavorings, then in the egg and finally in the panko.

Fill a frying pan with oil and turn on the flame, when the oil is hot, fry the chicken until golden brown, then let stand for about 5 minutes.

In a saucepan bring water to a boil and cook eggs for 5 minutes, then run them under cold water, peel and marinate 10 minutes in a container with soy sauce.

Cook the noodles directly in the broth for 3 minutes or according to the directions on the package.

Divide the broth and noodles among bowls, add the fried chicken, sauce, and halved eggs.

Ramen Sandwich with Chicken

Servings: 2   **Preparation Time: 25 minutes**

400 g ramen noodles
3 tablespoons olive or seed oil

300 g chopped chicken breast
1 spring onion

2 eggs
2 tablespoons teriyaki sauce

Directions

In a small saucepan, bring water to a boil and cook the noodles for 3 minutes or according to the directions on the package. When ready drain them, pour them into a bowl, add the previously beaten eggs and mix well.

Heat two tablespoons of oil in a frying pan and, when hot, pour in half of the noodles, giving them the shape of an omelet. Cook for about 3 minutes; the noodles should brown and become crispy. Once this time has passed, with the help of a lid, turn the noodle disk over and cook it on the other side as well. When it is crispy, remove it from the pan and repeat Directions with the other half.

When finished, in the same pan, add another tablespoon of oil and cook the chicken breasts 4 minutes per side. Remove and set aside.

Compose this dish as if it were a sandwich, placing the meat, thinly sliced spring onion and teriyaki sauce between the two noodle discs.

Cut into slices and enjoy while still warm.

Tonkotsu Saffron Ramen

Servings: 2   **Preparation Time: 2 hours and 15 minutes**

300 g ramen noodles
2000 ml Tonkotsu broth
1 pork loin of at least 250 g

2 tablespoons of seed or olive oil
3 tablespoons of soy sauce

2 spring onions
A few sprigs of chives
1 dose of saffron
40 g of soybean sprouts

Directions

Heat two tablespoons of oil in a saucepan; when it has reached the correct temperature, lay the pork loin inside and brown it 2 minutes on each side so that it seals evenly. Once this step is done pour in all the broth, close with the lid, turn the heat down to low and let it cook for at least 2 hours. After this time has elapsed, take the meat out and let it rest for a few minutes before cutting it into thin slices.

Add soy sauce to add more flavor to the dish.

Cut the spring onion into very thin strips and finely chop the chives.

Soak saffron in a glass of hot water for about 3 minutes, use half of it immediately to flavor the broth and the remainder to garnish the dish.

Bring water to a boil in a saucepan and cook the noodles inside for 3 minutes or according to the directions on the package. When ready, drain them and divide them into bowls.

Lay the loin slices on the rim of the bowls and pour the broth inside until the noodles are completely covered. Top the dish with a generous dollop of spring onion, soybean sprouts, chives, and the remaining saffron pistils.

Miso Ramen with Mushroom Chicken

Servings: 2   **Preparation Time: 20 minutes**

300 g ramen noodle
200 g chicken breast
600 ml miso broth
1 onion
3 slices of ginger

1 clove of garlic
4 tablespoons seed or olive oil
10 tablespoons soy sauce
1 spring onion

100 g fresh mushrooms to taste
2 eggs

Directions

Finely chop the onion, ginger and garlic and sauté them in a pan with a little oil. Pour over 2 tablespoons of soy sauce, the broth and bring to a boil.

Cook the noodles in boiling water for 3 minutes or according to the instructions on the package.

Mince the spring onion. Clean and fry the mushrooms in a pan with 2 tablespoons of hot oil. Marinade the chicken breast with 3 tablespoons soy sauce and cook it in the same pan as the mushrooms.

Boil the eggs for 5 minutes and then first put them in ice water and, once cold, shell them and marinate in the remaining soy sauce.

Arrange the noodles in serving bowls, then pour in the broth and add the rest of the ingredients. Enjoy this dish while still hot.

Ramen in Chicken and Black Garlic Broth

Servings: 2   **Preparation Time: 1 hour and 20 minutes**

300 g ramen noodles
4 slices of bacon
1 egg
2 tablespoons of soy sauce

1 tablespoon chopped cilantro
10 g gari
For the broth
4 liters of water,
2 over chicken thighs

100 ml sake
2 cloves of black garlic
20 g of ginger
3 carrots
1 celery stalk
1 spring onion

Directions

Prepare the broth by putting all the ingredients in a pot of cold water. Before adding the vegetables, clean them and cut them into coarse pieces, as they will be the crunchy part dish. After about an hour, take a tablespoon of broth and mix it with the soy sauce in a bowl.

Boil water in a saucepan and cook the egg with the whole shell for 5 minutes. Remove the shell and marinate it in the broth and soy mixture.

Heat a skillet and brown the bacon slices until crispy on top, then lay them in the broth. At this point cook the noodles directly in the broth for a few minutes. Serve in bowls with broth, noodles, one egg, vegetables, shredded chicken and bacon. Garnish with the cilantro and gari.

Shoyu Ramen with Double Cooked Chicken

Servings: 2   **Preparation Time: 1 hour**

300 g ramen noodles
300 g chicken pieces
600 ml of shoyu broth
1 egg
1 onion

40 g of soybean sprouts
100 g spinach
1 tablespoon of sesame seeds

1 tablespoon oyster sauce
1 tablespoon seed or olive oil
Soy sauce to taste

Directions

To prepare this dish start by heating the Shoyu broth, adding from the start a tablespoon of oyster sauce and if you like also a tablespoon of soy sauce.

Pour the chicken pieces directly into the broth and continue cooking for about 40 minutes, after this time has elapsed remove it from the broth, heat a tablespoon of oil in a frying pan and sauté the chicken for about 15 minutes. This second cooking will serve to make it crispier and more flavorful.

In a saucepan, bring water to a boil and cook the egg inside for 5 minutes. Once ready, drain it, shell it and leave it to marinate in the soy sauce.

Bring water to a boil and cook the noodles inside for 3 minutes or according to the directions on the package. When they are cooked, drain and divide them into bowls.

Assemble the dish by filling the bowls with the broth to cover the noodles, add the chicken, soybean sprouts, chopped onion, chopped spinach, and egg cut in half. Garnish with the sesame seeds.

Ramen in Double Broth and Pork Tenderloin

Servings: 4   **Preparation Time: 3 hours**

600 g ramen noodles
8 shiitake mushrooms
1 tablespoon of seed oil
1 pork tenderloin
3 tablespoons of soy sauce

50 ml rice wine
2 spring onions
10 g grated ginger
2 sheets of nori seaweed
For the broth
1 whole chicken

1 leek
1 onion
2 cloves of fresh garlic
3 slices of fresh ginger
2 carrots

Directions

Put the chicken, leek, onion, two cloves of garlic, ginger and two carrots in cold water, cover completely with cold water. Bring everything to a boil and cook for at least 3 hours. The longer it is boiled, the better. Once ready strain it.

In a skillet, preferably nonstick, pour 1 tablespoon of oil and briefly brown the pork tenderloin on all sides until golden brown. When it is ready, place it in a large pot, pour in the soy sauce and 50 ml of rice wine. Add the sliced spring onion and grated ginger. Pour water over it so that the tenderloin is almost completely covered with liquid. Bring the liquid to a boil. Remove the tenderloin after 30 minutes and set aside. Cut the pork into slices about 5 mm thick and add it back to its broth, adding the sliced mushrooms.

While the broth and meat finish cooking, take the opportunity to cook the noodles as well. In a saucepan bring water to a boil and cook them for 3 minutes or for the time indicated on the package. When ready drain them and set them aside.

When the chicken broth is ready, put it in a pot with the pork broth and season with a few tablespoons of soy sauce. Cut the nori seaweed sheets into small strips.

Pour the noodles into bowls and cover with the chicken and pork broth. Garnish with two or three slices of pork, the nori seaweed strips, and a finely chopped spring onion.

Ramen with Chicken and Chili Broth

Servings: 4   **Preparation Time: 2 hours**

600 g ramen noodles   *1 fresh spring onion*   *Carrots 3*
4 eggs   *1 fresh chili pepper*   *Onions 2*
400 g chicken breast   *2 tablespoons honey*   *Fresh ginger 5 slices*
6 tablespoons of soy   *4 tablespoons soy*
sauce   **For the chicken broth**   *sauce*
3 tablespoons sesame   *Chicken pieces, about*
seeds   *600 g*

Directions

To prepare this dish, the first thing to do is to make the chicken broth. To have a rich and flavorful broth, the secret is to cook it a lot over a low flame; about two hours are needed. In a pot filled with cold water pour the chicken cut into pieces, all the vegetables washed and roughly chopped, and the rest of the stock ingredients. Turn the heat on low and let it cook for about two hours.

Meanwhile in a saucepan of water you can prepare the eggs. Bring it to a boil and dip the eggs in it for about 4 minutes (more if you like the yolk well cooked). Once cooked, remove the skins and marinate them in about 4 tablespoons of soy sauce.

Now take care of the chicken breast, cut it into strips about 1 cm thick and put it in a bowl. Pour in the rest of the soy sauce and honey and mix thoroughly.

Heat a frying pan, when hot, cook the chicken breast 3 minutes per side, also flavor it with sesame seeds while it is cooking.

In a saucepan bring water to a boil and cook the noodles. Once ready you can plate the dish.

In a bowl pour the noodles first, then the broth and chicken. Top the dish with the egg cut in half and the finely chopped chili and spring onion.

Shoyu with Beef Steak

Servings: 2   **Preparation Time: 20 minutes**

300 g ramen noodles
600 ml of shoyu broth
1 beef steak of at least 200 g
1 tablespoon of seed or olive oil

1 spring onion
1 tablespoon of sake
5 tablespoons of soy sauce
20 g chopped ginger

1 tablespoon oyster sauce
2 eggs

Directions

Pour a tablespoon of oil into a large skillet and brown the spring onion (finely chopped) for a few minutes, turning constantly to prevent it from burning. Pour the broth, sake and soy sauce into the pan. Add the ginger and oyster sauce.

Take a grill pan, let it heat over high heat for a minute and cook the meat 2 minutes per side so that it remains pink in the center. You can increase the cooking time if you prefer it well done. Remove it from the grill pan, let it rest a few minutes and cut it into slices about 1 cm thick.

Boil the eggs for 5 minutes, peel and marinate 10 minutes in the soy sauce. In a saucepan, bring water to a boil and cook noodles for 3 minutes or according to package directions.

Divide noodles among bowls, cover with broth, add meat and eggs cut in half.

Ramen with Spiced Pork Belly

Servings: 2   **Preparation Time: 30 minutes**

300 g ramen noodles
800 ml tonkotsu broth
1 piece of bacon about 200 g

1 tablespoon of olive or seed oil
30 g of soybean sprouts
1 tablespoon of sesame paste

1 sheet of kombu seaweed
½ spring onion
1 pinch of black pepper

Directions

Cook the bacon directly in the broth over low heat for about 1 hour.

After this time has elapsed, remove the meat and strain the broth through a fine strainer. Pat the bacon dry with a paper towel and cut it into slices.

In a separate pot bring water to a boil and cook the noodles for 3 minutes.

Heat a tablespoon of oil in a skillet and brown the bacon over high heat on all sides.

Add the kombu and sesame paste to the broth, stir well to let all the flavors blend.

Drain the pasta and divide it into bowls, add the browned bacon and fill with the broth. Garnish with spring onion, soybean sprouts and a pinch of black pepper.

Ramen with Spicy Chicken

Servings: 4   **Preparation Time: 1 hour and 10 minutes**

600 g ramen noodles

500 g chicken breast

1 tablespoon of soy sauce

1 tablespoon of honey

1 tablespoon olive or seed oil

1 fresh chili pepper

1 fresh shallot

1 tablespoon sesame seeds

For the Broth

About 500 g chicken pieces

2 Carrots

1 Onion

5 slices of fresh ginger

1 tablespoon of sweet paprika

Directions

Start the recipe by preparing the broth: put the chicken, peeled carrot, peeled onion, chopped fresh ginger and paprika in a large pot. Cover everything with cold water, bring to a boil and cook for about 1 hour. When cooked, strain the broth and add soy sauce until the desired taste is achieved.

Concentrate now on preparing the actual ramen. Cut the chicken breast into strips about 1 cm thick, saute in a pan with soy sauce, extra virgin olive oil and a tablespoon of honey. Cook for about 8 minutes stirring occasionally, once cooked turn off the flame and let it rest for a few minutes.

Separately, bring a saucepan full of water to a boil and cook the noodles. Drain them when al dente (about 3 minutes cooked) and cool them immediately under running water, set aside until ready to serve.

Cut the chili and shallots into thin slices.

Lay the noodles in a bowl divided by portion, add the sliced chicken, chili, and shallots, then pour in the broth until everything is covered. Garnish with sesame seeds toasted in a pan for 2 minutes.

Shio Ramen with Turkey and Mushroom

Servings: 2   **Preparation Time: 30 minutes**

300 g ramen noodles
600 ml Shio broth
200 g turkey breast
1 tablespoon miso paste

3 tablespoons seed or olive oil
2 eggs
100 g chiodini mushrooms

1 fresh chili pepper
1 spring onion
15 g chopped ginger
1 tablespoon of soy sauce

Directions

Cut the turkey pieces into thin strips, mix them with miso paste and 1 tablespoon of oil, and let them marinate for about 10 minutes. You can also marinate them a few hours ahead to let them take on more flavor.

Cook the eggs in boiling water for 5 minutes, remove them from the water, let them cool, peel them and cut them in half.

Cut the mushrooms and spring onion into strips and the chili pepper into thin slices. Heat 2 tablespoons of oil in a fairly large skillet, brown the spring onion and chili well for a couple of minutes, then add the mushrooms.

Move the mushrooms to the edge of the pan and cook the turkey strips in the center to let the flavors blend well.

Add the broth, ginger and soy sauce at this point as well. Let cook another 15 minutes on high heat.

In a saucepan bring water to a boil, cook the noodles inside for 3 minutes or according to the directions on the package. Drain and divide them into bowls.

Pour over the soup with the turkey until coated. Serve while still hot.

Ramen in Carbonara Style

Servings: 2   **Preparation Time: 30 minutes**

300 g ramen noodles   *100 g pork belly*   *1 pinch of black pepper*
2 eggs   *1 clove of garlic (to taste)*
Directions

In a small bowl, crack the eggs open and beat them with a whisk until smooth.

Cut the bacon into cubes of about half an inch and cook them in a frying pan over medium heat until crispy, it will take about 10 minutes. It is very important to continuously turn the bacon par get it to cook evenly. At the beginning of cooking you can add a clove of minced garlic if you like.

In a saucepan, bring water to a boil and cook the noodles for 3 minutes or according to the directions on the package.

We have now reached the decisive step in this recipe; it is important that you follow the directions to the letter. Remove the noodles and water from the pot. Return the noodles to the pot while still hot, add the bacon and beaten eggs. Turn the noodles continuously with a spoon; the heat from the pot and noodles will be transferred to the eggs, making them creamy. After about 2 minutes remove them, divide them into bowls, add a pinch of black pepper and enjoy them while still hot.

Chicken Ramen with Aromatic Sauce

Servings: 2   **Preparation Time: 3 hours and 10 minutes**

300 g ramen noodles
2 eggs
6 tablespoons of soy sauce
40 ml of sake

2 scallions
10 g fresh chopped ginger
For the broth
1 kg chicken pieces

4 liters of water
1 carrot
1 leek
1 clove of garlic
3 slices of ginger

Directions

For the broth, soak roughly cut chicken, carrot, leek, garlic and ginger in cold water, turn on and cook for about 3 hours. After this time has elapsed, remove the chicken from the broth and let it cool slightly. Remove the meat from the bones and cut it into pieces.

Boil the eggs in a saucepan, after 5 minutes remove them from the water, let them cool, shell them, and let them marinate in half the soy sauce.

In a saucepan heat the remaining soy sauce, sake, one shallot cut into rings, and finely chopped ginger for 5 minutes. Add the chicken meat and cook over low heat with the lid closed for about 10 minutes. Add about 600 ml of broth (strained) and continue to cook over low heat.

In another pot of boiling water cook the noodles for 5 minutes or according to package directions.

When ready divide them into bowls, pour the meat-flavored broth, ginger and halved eggs over them, top with the meat and garnish with the remaining scallion rings.

Ramen with Spicy Beef Steak

Servings: 2   **Preparation Time: 20 minutes**

2 beef steaks of at least 150 g each
1 tablespoon of oil
1 pinch of black pepper
1 tablespoon teriyaki sauce

300 g ramen noodles
200 g precooked beans
800 ml tonkotsu broth
1 tablespoon chili sauce
½ red onion cut into thin slices

1 tablespoon chopped cilantro
1 fresh chili pepper
½ lime

Directions

Heat a frying pan or griddle. Brush the steaks with oil, salt and pepper to taste. Place them in the skillet and cook for 2 minutes per side so that they will be well cooked on the outside but still rare inside. Remove them from the pan and let them rest for a few minutes. Brush the steaks with the teriyaki sauce and cut them into slices about 1 cm thick.

Meanwhile, cook the noodles in a pot of boiling water for 3 minutes.

Blanch the beans in a large pot of boiling water for 10 minutes; drain and cool under cold running water.

Heat the broth in a pot and add the chili sauce. Divide the noodles into bowls, pour off the broth and add the beef slices and beans. Finally, add the red onion, chopped cilantro leaves, chili and lime slices.

Spicy Tantanmen Ramen with Spinach

Servings: 2   **Preparation Time: 25 minutes**

800 ml of shoyu broth
300 g ramen noodles
200 g ground pork
½ onion
3 slices of fresh ginger

1 tablespoon of olive or seed oil
1 fresh chili pepper
100 ml of sake
150 g spinach

1 box of soybean sprouts
2 tablespoons of sesame paste
1 tablespoon of soy sauce

Directions

Chop the onion and ginger, put them in a pan greased with oil and sauté. Add the ground meat and brown it, turning it continuously for the first few minutes with a wooden spoon. When the color of the meat turns white, add the sliced chili and sauté well for a few minutes, then add the sake, stir and brown again over a high flame for 2-3 minutes, letting all the alcohol evaporate.

Boil spinach leaves for 2-3 minutes in boiling water and drain. Put soybean sprouts in a colander and pour boiling water over them.

Heat the shoyu broth. Meanwhile, cook noodles in boiling water for 3 minutes. Take bowls and put 1 tablespoon sesame paste and 1/2 teaspoon soy sauce in each. Pour about 400 ml of hot broth into each bowl and mix well. Add the noodles and later the rest of the ingredients. Serve hot.

Shio Ramen with Sweet and Sour Pork Belly

Servings: 2   **Preparation Time: 1 hour and 15 minutes**

300 g ramen noodles
600 ml Shio broth
1 piece of pork belly of at least 200 g

4 tablespoons of honey
2 eggs
4-5 slices of fresh ginger

4 tablespoons of soy sauce
40 g of soybean sprouts
A few sprigs of chives

Directions

The first thing to do is to boil the bacon 10 minutes in water, to which you will have added ginger slices, so as to remove the flavor of the fat. Having done this brief step, spread the honey on the meat and bake it in the oven at 220° for about 1 hour. After this time has elapsed turn off the oven, but leave the meat inside so that it does not undergo abrupt changes in temperature.

As soon as you have placed the bacon back in the oven, boil the eggs for about 5 minutes. When they are ready, remove them from the water, wait for them to cool, peel them, and let them marinate in the soy sauce. Heat the broth.

In a saucepan, bring water to a boil and cook the noodles for 3 minutes or according to the directions on the package. Once ready, remove them from the water and set aside.

Divide the noodles into bowls and cover them with the broth you have previously set to heat for at least 5 minutes. Cut the bacon into slices and lay them in the bowls, along with the egg cut in half. Top the dish with the soybean sprouts and chopped chives.

Fish Ramen

Miso Ramen with Spicy Prawns

Servings: 2   **Preparation Time: 1 hour and 10 minutes**

300 g ramen noodles
1000 ml Miso broth
10 shrimps
2 tablespoons seed or olive oil

1 pinch of black pepper
1 pinch of chopped chili pepper
2 eggs

2 tablespoons of soy sauce
30 g or so of edamame
1 tablespoon of sesame seeds

Directions

Let's start by first preparing the shrimp. Wash them well under running water, remove the head, carapace and tails. Place them in a bowl, season them with 1 tablespoon of oil, soy sauce, pepper and chili, mix them so that all the ingredients are blended and let them rest in the refrigerator for about 1 hour. This way the shrimp will flavor and be tastier.

After this time has elapsed, take a frying pan, better still a wok, and heat 1 tablespoon of oil inside it. Pour in the shrimp and cook them over high heat for 3 minutes, turning them continuously to prevent them from burning. Once cooked remove them from the pan and set aside. In the same skillet add the edamame, saute them for a couple of minutes and set them aside as well. Use the same one to toast the sesame seeds as well.

Boil one pot of water to cook the noodles and another to cook the eggs. Remember that the noodles will need to cook 3 minutes if you are using fresh noodles, about twice as long if you are using dry noodles; the eggs, on the other hand, will need 5 minutes to cook.

If the broth is cold, take advantage of this time to bring it to a boil.

When the pasta is ready, you can compose the dish. In a bowl, pour the broth, lay the noodles on the bottom, followed by the shrimp, edamame and eggs cut in half. Top with the toasted sesame seeds and enjoy hot.

Shio Ramen with Shrimp, Basil and Lemon

Servings: 2   **Preparation Time: 1 hour and 10 minutes**

300 g ramen noodles	*2 tablespoons seed or olive oil*	*1 red bell pepper*
1000 ml Shio broth		*4 slices of ginger*
10 shrimps	*½ onion*	*1 clove of fresh garlic, minced*
10 fresh basil leaves	*Juice of 1 lemon*	
1 pinch of black pepper	*2 tablespoons soy sauce*	*50 g fresh spinach*

Directions

Take a nonstick frying pan or wok and put it on the stove over a fairly high flame. Heat 1 tablespoon of oil and pour the washed and shelled shrimp inside. Add the washed and roughly chopped basil leaves, salt and black pepper; they should cook about one minute per side. Once ready transfer them to a plate.

In the same skillet cook the spinach for 3 minutes; once ready set aside.

Still using the same pan (you will intensify the flavor this way) now pour in the diced onion and bell bell pepper and cook for about 3 minutes, turning occasionally to prevent sticking. Add the ginger slices and chopped garlic and continue cooking for another 2 minutes.

Add the broth and bring everything to a boil. Separately put a saucepan with water on the stove and cook the noodles for 3 minutes (6 minutes in case you are using dry noodles).

When everything is ready, compose the dish by pouring the broth first, then the noodles and shrimp and finally adding 1 tablespoon of soy sauce, the juice of ½ lemon and the spinach.

Ramen with Mullet and Shrimp

Servings: 2   **Preparation Time: 2 hours and 30 minutes**

300 g ramen noodles
6 shrimps
1 tablespoon of seed or olive oil
1 tablespoon of soy sauce

1 pinch of pepper
For the broth
3 Liters of water
6 mullets
2 sheets of nori seaweed

1 spring onion
1 carrot
2 g katsuobushi

Directions

To prepare this delicious dish, the first thing you will need to do is clean the mullet. To do this you will have to cut off the belly, remove the innards, later cut off the head and tail and remove the center bone. This sounds very complicated, but I assure you that it is actually a very simple Directions.

Now you need to start making the broth because it is quite a long preparation, plus the longer it is on the stove, the tastier it will become. To make the broth, pour cold water into a pot along with the bones and heads of the mullet, nori seaweed, a peeled and roughly cut carrot, katsoubushi, chopped spring onion and a pinch of salt. Turn on the heat and let it cook for about 2 hours.

While you are waiting for the broth to be ready, take a frying pan and heat 1 tablespoon of oil. When the oil is hot, place the mullet fillets on the skin side and let them cook 1 minute, turn them over and cook another 30 seconds. Remove them from the heat and set them aside. In the same hot pan pour the shrimp, which you will have previously shelled, and cook them 1 minute per side.

After about 2 hours the broth will be ready, at which point remove the fish and vegetables, strain the broth through a strainer and return it to the heat for another 30 minutes.

After 30 minutes pour in the ramen noodles and cook them 3 minutes. Turn off the heat and serve them by adding the fish, soy sauce and a pinch of black pepper to the dish.

Ramen with Shrimp and Cabbage

Servings: 2

Preparation Time: 2 hours

2 tablespoons of soy sauce
300 g ramen noodles
10 g grated ginger
150 g fresh cabbage
1 tablespoon seed or olive oil
1 chili pepper
1 tablespoon honey

1 clove of fresh garlic
1 orange
For the broth
5 liters of cold water
1 orange
2 tablespoons oyster sauce or 4 fresh oysters (just the shellfish)
1 tablespoon honey

3 slices of fresh ginger
1 tablespoon paprika
1 sheet of nori seaweed
1 tablespoon miso paste
1 clove of fresh garlic
200 g shrimp

Directions

Start with the broth. In a large pot with 5 liters of cold water squeeze one orange, add the soy sauce, oyster sauce, 1 tablespoon honey, ginger, paprika, nori seaweed sheet, miso paste and 2 crushed garlic cloves and simmer for at least 2 hours. After this time strain it and put it back on the stove on a low flame until the end of the recipe.

Clean the shrimp under running water, remove the carapace and soak them in the broth for 5 minutes, after which remove and set aside.

In a pan, cook the remaining honey, soy sauce, grated ginger, a crushed clove of garlic, orange slices and their juice until a very tasty syrup is obtained. Add the shrimp and cook for another 5 minutes.

In another pot of boiling water, cook the noodles for 3 minutes or according to package directions. When they are done, drain and set aside.

Wash the cabbage, cut it into thin slices, and saute for 3 minutes in a skillet with 1 tablespoon of oil and, if desired, a chili pepper.

Divide the noodles into bowls, cover with the hot broth, and finish this tasty fish ramen with the spicy shrimp and spicy cabbage.

Ramen with Shrimp and Squid

Servings: 2   **Preparation Time: 20 minutes**

300 g ramen noodles   *200 g squid*   *2 tablespoons of soy*
600 ml miso broth   *1 fresh spring onion*   *sauce*
150 g of shrimp   *20 g wakame seaweed*   *6 slices of narutomaki*
Directions

Very simple recipe but at the same time quick (if you have already prepared the broth, maybe the day before) and tasty.

In a saucepan full of boiling water, cook the ramen noodles for 3 minutes or according to the time indicated on the package, once ready drain and set aside.

Boil the strained broth, add the cleaned shrimp, squid cut into rounds and let it cook for about 15 minutes.

Divide the noodles into two bowls, pour the fish-flavored broth over them, and add the narutomaki slices, wakame seaweed, soy sauce, and finely sliced spring onion.

Ramen with Salmon, quick preparation

Servings: 2   **Preparation Time: 20 minutes**

300 g ramen noodles
2 fillets of Norwegian salmon
2 eggs
1 tablespoon of seed oil

1 spring onion
1 fresh chili pepper
4 tablespoons soy sauce
For the broth
2 tablespoons miso paste

4 tablespoons soy sauce
1000 ml water
6 dried shiitake mushrooms
1 tablespoon of ginger

Directions

First prepare the broth. Put the miso paste and soy sauce in a pot and cover with cold water (about 1000 ml). Bring to a boil, then add the mushrooms and ginger. Cook for about 7 to 10 minutes until the mushrooms are cooked.

While the broth is boiling, prepare the eggs. Bring a pot of water to a boil and cook the eggs inside for 5 minutes. Remove them from the pot and run them under cold water before peeling them. Let them marinate in the soy sauce until ready to serve.

Now deal with the salmon. Remove all the bones from the fillets and cut them in half for easy cooking. Heat the seed oil in a large frying pan and lay the salmon in it, skin side down. Cook over high heat for about 3 minutes, then turn the fillets over and cook for another minute. Increase the cooking time by a few minutes if you want the fish more cooked through, but be careful not to overcook or it will become tough.

Add the noodles to the broth and simmer for 1-2 minutes until cooked through. Divide them between two bowls. Cover with broth and mushrooms. Top the dish with the eggs cut in half, spring onion and chopped chili.

Ramen with Lime-Scented Shrimp

Servings: 2   **Preparation Time: 2 hours**

300 g ramen noodles
6 tablespoons of soy sauce
3 slices of fresh ginger
1 tablespoon of sake
1 lime
200 g shrimp

1 egg
1 fresh cilantro branch finely chopped
For the broth
5 liters of water
1 shallot
2 tablespoons sesame oil

1 clove of garlic
1 tablespoon miso paste
3 slices of fresh ginger
1 tablespoon of sake
1 zucchini

Directions

Prepare the broth by sautéing shallots in 1 tablespoon sesame oil, garlic, miso paste, half the soy sauce, 3 slices of ginger, and stirring in 1 tablespoon sake in a pot. At this point add water and leave on the stove for 2 hours.

Also cut a zucchini into slices and combine with the broth.

In a saucepan filled with boiling water, cook ramen noodles for 3 minutes or according to the time indicated on the package, once ready drain and set aside.

Shell the shrimp and cook them in a pan for about 5 minutes with a drizzle of sesame oil, ginger, 2 tablespoons of soy sauce and sake, once ready set them aside.

Prepare the egg so that the white is firm and the yolk should be creamy. To do this, soak it in a saucepan of boiling water for 5 minutes. Let it cool, peel it and keep it covered in the remaining soy sauce until it is time to serve.

At this point divide the noodles into bowls. Add the shrimp to the broth and turn up the heat for a couple of minutes, add a dash of lime juice and pour it into the bowls until the noodles are covered. Top with the egg cut in half and fresh cilantro.

Ramen with Shrimp in Rum

Servings: 2   **Preparation Time: 40 minutes**

300 g ramen noodles   *200 g shrimp*   *2 tablespoons of sake*
2 eggs   *50 ml rum*   *1 clove of fresh garlic*
2 carrots   **For the broth**   *25 g fresh ginger*
60 g daikon   *5 liters of water*
1 tablespoon of seed or   *1 tablespoon of soy sauce*
olive oil   *1 tablespoon miso*

Directions

Put a large pot on the stove, pour in the water, soy sauce, miso, sake, garlic and fresh grated ginger, stir and cook over medium heat for about 30 minutes.

Cook the eggs for 5 minutes in a saucepan of boiling water, this way you will get the yolk creamy but the albumen well cooked. Remove them from the saucepan and set aside to cool. In this dish I prefer to leave them like this, but if you prefer you can marinate them in soy sauce.

Wash the carrots and daikon, slice both and set aside.

In a saucepan full of boiling water cook the noodles for 3 minutes or according to the time indicated on the package, once ready drain and set aside.

In a frying pan heat 1 tablespoon of oil, cook the shrimp, which you have previously cleaned and shelled, for 2 minutes, and deglaze with 1 glass of rum over high heat. Cook another 3 minutes (this way all the alcohol will evaporate) and set aside.

Divide the noodles into bowls, add the broth until it covers them, and complete the ramen by adding the shrimp, eggs, and vegetables.

Miso Ramen with Boiled Salmon

Servings: 2   **Preparation Time: 20 minutes**

300 g ramen noodles
600 ml Miso broth
2 salmon fillets of about
100 g each
1 spring onion

1 clove of fresh garlic
3 slices of fresh ginger
100 g chiodini mushrooms

2 tablespoons of seed or olive oil
1 tablespoon of sesame seeds

Directions

Toast the sesame in a skillet, turning it constantly, transfer it to a bowl and set aside.

Clean the spring onion and cut it into thin slices. Cut the salmon fillets into strips about 1 cm thick. Cut and finely chop the garlic and ginger.

Heat two tablespoons of oil in a pot and brown the mushrooms, which you will have thinly sliced. Add the garlic, spring onion, and ginger and sauté the mixture, being careful to stir constantly to prevent it from burning.

Add the broth and cook for about 5 minutes, add the salmon and continue cooking another 5 minutes until it is cooked.

In a saucepan, bring water to a boil and cook the noodles for 3 minutes or according to the directions on the package. Once ready, remove them from the water and set aside.

Divide the noodles into bowls, cover with the broth, fish, and sauteed mushrooms. Garnish with the toasted sesame seeds.

Ramen with Spicy Cod

Servings: 2   **Preparation Time: 40 minutes**

800 ml fish broth
300 g ramen noodles
1 tablespoon miso paste
2 tablespoons of mirin

2 tablespoons of soy sauce
4 tablespoons of sesame oil

20 g grated ginger
250 g cod fillets
100 g cabbage
1 fresh chili pepper

Directions

In a large bowl pour 1 tablespoon miso paste, 2 tablespoons mirin, 1 tablespoon soy sauce, 1 tablespoon sesame oil, and grated ginger. Mix well until smooth, add the cod fillets and let marinate for at least 30 minutes.

Heat 2 tablespoons of oil in a skillet over medium heat and cook the fillets with the skin side down. Let the fish cook for 2-3 minutes until the skin turns golden brown, then flip and cook for another 2-3 minutes on the other side. Transfer the cod to a plate and set aside.

In a saucepan filled with boiling water, cook the noodles for 3 minutes or according to the time indicated on the package, once ready drain and set aside.

Add the remaining oil to the same pan and sauté the cabbage (cut into strips) until it starts to wilt.

Pour the fish stock into the pan, add a tablespoon of soy sauce and bring to a boil.

Divide the noodles into two bowls and cover with the broth. Add the cod and garnish with sliced chilli

.

Ramen with Cod and Mushrooms

Servings: 2   **Preparation Time: 2 hours**

300 g ramen noodle
1 carrot
40 g of soybean sprouts
2 tablespoons of seed or olive oil
100 g clove mushrooms

1 egg
150 g of cod fillets
1 tablespoon of soy sauce
For the broth
5 liters of water
1 onion

1 celery stalk
1 leek
1 clove of fresh garlic
1 carrot

Directions

Clean the onion and cut it into thin slices. Wash and chop the celery and leek. Mince the garlic. Clean the carrots and cut one into slices and the other into strips. Prepare a stock with all the cleaned vegetables (except the carrot strips), boiling them in about 5 liters of water for 2 hours.

Boil a pot of salted water and cook the noodles for 3 minutes or according to the directions on the package, drain and set aside.

In a skillet pour 1 tablespoon of oil and cook the mushrooms for 10 minutes, once ready set aside. In the same skillet saute the carrots cut into strips and the soybean sprouts for 5 minutes.

In a pot of boiling water cook the egg for 5 minutes, drain and let it cool before peeling.

Pour a tablespoon of oil into a nonstick skillet, add the cod fillet and cook until golden brown on both sides, always starting with the skin side.

Divide the noodles into bowls, cover with the hot broth, and add the cod, egg cut in half, mushrooms, vegetables, and a tablespoon of soy sauce to taste.

Ramen with Cod in Shio Broth

Servings: 1   **Preparation Time: 30 minutes**

300 ml Shio broth   *1 clove of garlic*   *1 tablespoon of sake*
100 g of cod fillet   *1 tablespoon miso*
150 g ramen noodle   *15 g grated ginger*
Directions

Salt the cod and bake it in the oven at 175 degrees for 5 minutes.

Heat 300 ml of broth in a pot and add the miso. Once dissolved, add the grated ginger, garlic and sake.

Boil a pot of salted water and cook the noodles for 3 minutes or according to the directions on the package, drain and set aside.

Pour the broth into a bowl, then add the noodles and codfish.

Shoyu Ramen with Shrimp Tempura

Servings: 2   **Preparation Time: 30 minutes**

300 g ramen noodles
600 ml of shoyu broth
4-6 shrimps
1 liter of seed oil for frying

1 spring onion
40 g of soybean buds
1 tablespoon chopped cilantro

For the tempura
100 g 00 flour
100 g rice flour
150 ml water
About 100 g ice

Directions

The first thing to do is to clean the shrimp; to do this, first remove the head and then the carapace, taking care to also extract the central gut, which is not pleasant to eat. Prepare the tempura by mixing the flours and then the ice and water. Shake vigorously until the mixture is smooth and lumpy.

Fill a frying pan with seed oil and heat until hot enough to fry, usually about 4 minutes will be needed. Pour the shrimp into the tempura, stir well to make the mixture stick, and one at a time toss them into the hot oil. Let them cook for about 3 minutes until they are golden brown and crispy. Remove them from the pan and place them to dry on kitchen paper.

Heat the broth to a boil.

Bring water to a boil in a saucepan and cook the noodles inside for 3 minutes or according to the directions on the package. When ready, drain them and divide them into bowls.

Pour the hot broth into the bowls until the noodles are completely covered. Add the tempura shrimp and garnish with the soybean sprouts, sliced spring onion, and coarsely chopped cilantro.

Ramen with Sweet and Sour Tuna Fillets

Servings: 2   **Preparation Time: 30 minutes**

300 g ramen noodles
150 g tuna
2 tablespoons rice vinegar
4 tablespoons of soy sauce

Juice of ½ lime
10 g finely grated ginger
1 tablespoon honey
1 tablespoon seed oil
½ shallot finely chopped
1 tablespoon paprika

1 tablespoon sesame seeds
1 tablespoon mirin
1 tablespoon brown sugar
50 ml sake

Directions

Special variation of ramen in which the broth is replaced with a special seasoning.

To make the dressing combine rice vinegar, 2 tablespoons soy sauce, lime juice, ginger and honey in a bowl, mix until smooth, add 1 tablespoon oil and mix again.

Boil a pot of salted water and cook the noodles for 3 minutes or according to the directions on the package, drain and set aside.

Pour the sauce over the noodles, add the shallots and paprika and mix well. Garnish with sesame seeds. Cover until ready to serve.

Now prepare the teriyaki sauce. Combine the remaining soy sauce, mirin, brown sugar, and sake in a small saucepan over medium heat and bring to a boil. Turn down the heat and simmer the sauce for about 15 minutes, until it is thick enough.

Grease a baking dish with oil, lay the tuna fillets inside and brush them with the teriyaki glaze. Bake the fish at 180 °C for 10 minutes and then brush it again with the glaze. Bake it another 5 minutes, glaze it again, and then remove it from the oven. Combine the tuna fillets with the noodles and serve.

Ramen with Sweet and Sour Grilled Tuna

Servings: 2   **Preparation Time: 20 minutes**

300 g ramen noodles
150 g tuna
2 tablespoons rice vinegar
4 tablespoons of soy sauce

Juice of ½ lime
10 g finely grated ginger
1 tablespoon honey
1 tablespoon sesame oil
½ shallot finely chopped
1 bell bell pepper diced

1 tablespoon seed oil
1 tablespoon mirin
1 tablespoon brown sugar
50 ml sake

Directions

Alternative version of the previous recipe.

In a bowl combine the rice wine vinegar, soy sauce, lemon juice, ginger, and sugar. Mix thoroughly. Add the sesame oil and stir again.

Boil a pot of salted water and cook the noodles for 3 minutes or according to the directions on the package, drain, and set aside.

Pour the previously prepared sauce over the noodles, add the chopped shallots, diced bell bell pepper and mix well.

Now prepare the teriyaki sauce. Combine the remaining soy sauce, mirin, brown sugar and sake in a small saucepan over medium heat and bring to a boil. Turn down the heat and simmer the sauce for about 15 minutes, until it is thick enough.

Turn on the grill, let it warm up thoroughly. Meanwhile, grease the tuna fillets with seed oil and transfer them to the hot grill. Cook them 2 minutes on each side.

Combine the tuna fillets with the noodles and serve.

Shoyu Ramen with Spicy Salmon Baked in the Oven

Servings: 2   **Preparation Time: 20 minutes**

300 g ramen noodles
600 ml of shoyu broth
2 salmon fillets
25 g fresh grated ginger

1 tablespoon chopped dried chili pepper
1 tablespoon seed or olive oil

1 shallot, finely chopped
1 tablespoon sesame oil
1 tablespoon of soy sauce

Directions

Preheat the oven to 180 °C (350 °F). Lay the salmon fillets skin-side down in an oiled baking dish. In a small bowl, mix 15 g ginger, 1 tablespoon dried chili and 1 tablespoon oil, then rub the resulting mixture evenly over the salmon. Cover it with a sheet of baking paper and bake it for about 15 minutes. Remove from the oven, and set aside.

Boil a pot of salted water and cook the noodles for 3 minutes or according to the directions on the package, drain and set aside.

Put the broth, the white part of the shallot, and the rest of the ginger in a pot and bring to a boil. Add the sesame oil and soy sauce. Divide the hot broth between two bowls. Top with the noodles, salmon pieces, and finally the finely chopped shallots.

Ramen with Sautéed Tuna

Servings: 2   **Preparation Time: 15 minutes**

300 g ramen noodles   *1 tablespoon of seed or*   *1 chili pepper*
600 ml fish broth   *olive oil*   *1 tablespoon of soy sauce*
½ onion   *2 tuna slices of about 80*   *1 tablespoon of rice*
                                 g each   *vinegar*

Directions

In a small saucepan, bring water to a boil and cook the noodles for 3 minutes or according to the directions on the package. When ready, remove them from the water and set aside.

Cut ½ onion into thin slices and brown in a skillet with a tablespoon of oil until translucent, add tuna and cook 3 minutes per side.

Heat the broth, season it with chili, soy sauce, and rice vinegar. Pour the broth into a bowl and lay the noodles inside. Add the tuna and top the dish with ½ finely chopped onion.

Shrimp Ramen with Winter Vegetables

Servings: 2   **Preparation Time: 35 minutes**

300 g ramen noodle
200 g of shrimps
600 ml fish stock
150 g Brussels sprouts
150 g of daikon

3 slices of fresh ginger
1 clove of fresh garlic
2 tablespoons seed or olive oil

2 tablespoons of soy sauce
1 tablespoon of rice vinegar
1 tablespoon miso paste

Directions

Cook noodles in boiling water for 3 minutes or according to package instructions, drain and rinse with cold water.

Wash Brussels sprouts under running water and clean them by removing the white underside.

Wash the daikon, peel it and cut it into slices about 3 millimeters thick. Peel the ginger and cut it into very thin slices. Also peel the garlic and chop it.

In a pot pour a tablespoon of oil and sauté the daikon, ginger and garlic for a few minutes.

Add the broth, soy sauce, rice vinegar and miso and cook for about 10 minutes. After that time has elapsed, add the Brussels sprouts and continue cooking on low heat for another 20 minutes.

Shell the shrimp and cook them in a skillet with a tablespoon of oil, 2 minutes per side. It is very important not to overcook them or they will remain chewy.

Divide the noodles into bowls, cover them with the broth and complete the dish with the sautéed shrimp and vegetables.

Miso Ramen with Salmon and Cabbage

Servings: 2   **Preparation Time: 20 minutes**

600 ml of Miso broth
300 g ramen noodles
2 tbsp. olive or seed oil

200 g salmon
1 pinch of black pepper
1 fresh chili pepper

3 slices of fresh ginger
150 g cabbage

Directions

Start by cooking the salmon. Put a tablespoon of oil in a skillet and heat it over medium heat. When hot, lay the salmon in the pan with the skin side down and season with salt and pepper. Turn the salmon after 2 minutes, then continue cooking for another minute and finish it in the oven at 200 °C for another 5 minutes.

In another frying pan, heat a tablespoon of oil and add sliced chili pepper. When hot, add the cabbage cut into strips and cook for 3 minutes.

Add the ginger slices to the miso broth and bring it to a boil. Cook the noodles directly in it for 3 minutes or for the time indicated on the package.

When ready divide the broth and noodles into bowls and top the dish with the salmon and sautéed cabbage.

Vegetarian Ramen

Vegetarian Ramen with Carrots and Daikon

Servings: 2   **Preparation Time: 1 hour and 30 minutes**

300 g ramen noodles
1 leek
2 carrots
30 g daikon
2 eggs

5 tablespoons of soy sauce
2 fresh shiitake mushrooms

For the broth
3 liters of water
1 broccoli
3 carrots
2 tablespoons miso

Directions

Very intensely flavored recipe for true vegetable lovers!

In a pot pour about 3 liters of water. Wash the broccoli and separate the tops from the central part, which is too hard to eat. Wash 3 carrots, peel and slice them. Pour the vegetables into the pot, turn it on and let it cook on low heat for about an hour and a half. Just before it is ready, add the miso.

Slice the mushrooms and saute them in a nonstick pan for 3 minutes.

Wash the daikon, peel it and cut it into rounds. Cut the remaining carrots into long, thin sticks, also wash the leek, slice it and set it all aside, we will need it to garnish the dish at the end.

Bring a pot of water to a boil and cook the eggs inside for 5 minutes. Remove them from the pot and run them under cold water before peeling them. Let them marinate in the soy sauce until ready to serve.

Cook the noodles separately in boiling water for about 3 minutes. Once ready you can assemble the dish by serving the noodles with the broth, eggs, mushrooms and vegetables in a bowl.

Ramen with Seitan in Mushroom Broth

Servings: 2   **Preparation Time: 1 hour**

300 g ramen noodles
2 tablespoons olive or seed oil
1/2 onion
2 cloves of fresh garlic

1 small piece of fresh ginger
100 g fresh spinach
2 eggs
200 g seitan

For the broth
10 dried shiitake mushrooms
700 ml of water
2 of soy sauce

Directions

Begin preparation from the broth, which for this recipe will have mushrooms as the only ingredient. Soak the dried shiitake mushrooms in a medium-sized pot and cover with water. Bring the water to a boil and remove from the heat, leaving the mushrooms to soak for at least an hour.

Then remove them from the pot and cut them into slices about half an inch thick. Place the mushrooms with a cup of their water in an electric blender and blend until smooth. Pour this mixture into the remaining broth in the pot and add the soy sauce.

Heat a tablespoon of vegetable oil in a large skillet over medium heat. Finely chop the onion and add it to the pan, stirring often, until softened and slightly colored. Then add the minced garlic and sliced ginger and heat, stirring for a few more minutes. Remove from the heat and add the mixture to the pan with the broth.

In the same pan, brown the seitan (add a little oil if necessary) for a few minutes, turning often. Then remove it and set it aside.

Boil some water in a pot. Add spinach and cook for about a minute until slightly wilted. Remove and set aside.

Crack the eggs and dip them in the same boiling water, lower the heat and poach them for 4 minutes. Remove them and place them in a bowl until completely cool.

Put a pot with plenty of water on the stove to cook the noodles. Cook them for 3 minutes if you are using fresh noodles, otherwise for about twice as long.

While the noodles are cooking, take the opportunity to reheat the broth. When hot, add the miso and mirin and stir well.

Divide the noodles among the bowls and add the broth until it covers them. Add the spinach, seitan and poached egg to each bowl, being careful not to break it. Garnish with a slice of nori seaweed and coarsely chopped fresh chives.

Vegetarian Ramen with Stir-fried Vegetable Mix

Servings: 2   **Preparation Time: 20 minutes**

300 g ramen noodles
600 ml vegetable broth
6 dried shiitake mushrooms

2 carrots
150 g cabbage
2 eggs

1 tablespoon of seed or olive oil
40 g of soybean sprouts
1 spring onion

Directions

In a bowl of hot water, soak the mushrooms for at least 30 minutes. When they have softened, cut them into small pieces and set aside. Wash the carrots, peel and chop them into the shape you prefer. Wash and chop the cabbage, too.

In a frying pan heat a tablespoon of oil and pour in the vegetables. Cook over low heat for about 15 minutes, turning occasionally to prevent sticking.

When the vegetables have wilted, pour in all the broth and continue to heat.

Bring water to a boil and cook the eggs for about 5 minutes. When they are ready, remove them from the water, let them cool and peel them.

In a saucepan, bring water to a boil and cook the noodles for 3 minutes or according to package directions. When ready drain them and divide them into bowls.

Top the noodles with the broth and the vegetables inside, add the halved eggs, and garnish the dish with the soybean sprouts and sliced spring onion.

Ramen with Fried Egg

Servings: 2   **Preparation Time: 50 minutes**

300 g ramen noodles   *2 tablespoons olive or*   *1 fresh spring onion*
600 ml vegetable broth   *seed oil*   *A pinch of black pepper*
2 eggs   *1 potato*

Directions

Set the broth to heat. Wash the potato, peel it and place it inside the broth for about 40 minutes. After this time has elapsed, remove it and set it aside.

Heat oil in a frying pan, crack an egg inside it and cover with a lid. Let it cook for 3 minutes, turn off the flame and let it cool.

In a saucepan bring water to a boil and cook the noodles for 3 minutes or according to the directions on the package. When ready, remove them from the water and divide them into bowls. Pour the broth until they are covered, lay the egg and the potato cut in half on top. Top the dish with the sliced spring onion and a pinch of black pepper.

Ramen with Sweet and Sour Apple Seitan

Servings: 2   **Preparation Time: 1 hour and 15 minutes**

300 g ramen noodles   *30 g fresh ginger*   *1 apple*
600 ml vegetable broth   *2 cloves of garlic*   *2 eggs*
200 g seitan   *6 tablespoons of sake*   *1 tablespoon seed oil*
2 fresh chilies   *4 tablespoons soy sauce*

Directions

Finely chop the chili, ginger and garlic and put them in a bowl. Add half of the sake and soy sauce and mix well until smooth. Spread this paste evenly over the seitan and let it marinate for about one ra.

After this time has elapsed (you can leave it even longer), cook it in a pan for about 10 minutes.

In a saucepan of boiling water, cook the eggs for 5 minutes, remove them, cool them under running water, peel them and let them marinate in the soy sauce.

Cook noodles in boiling water for 3 minutes or according to package instructions, drain and rinse with cold water.

Peel the apple, remove the center core, and cut it into thin slices. Heat a tablespoon of seed oil in a skillet and saute for about 5 minutes. Halfway through cooking, deglaze with sake.

Divide the noodles into bowls, cover with the broth (which you will have previously warmed), add the seitan, halved eggs, and complete this delicious sweet-and-sour ramen with the apple blended with sake.

Ramen with Tofu and Daikon

Servings: 2   **Preparation Time: 20 minutes**

300 g ramen noodles
800 ml of vegetable broth
3 slices of ginger
1 clove of garlic
4 tablespoons of soy sauce

6 shiitake mushrooms
200 g tofu
1 tablespoon mirin
1 tablespoon sesame oil
1 egg
25 g daikon

1 tablespoon rice vinegar
1 tablespoon miso
100 g fresh spinach
1 fresh shallot

Directions

Heat broth and add ginger, garlic, 2 tablespoons soy sauce, mushrooms, and cook until boiling. Mix the remaining soy sauce and mirin with the tofu in a bowl. Let marinate for a few minutes. Next, pour the sesame oil into the pan, let it heat up and pour the tofu inside, cooking it until it becomes crispy.

Once ready set it aside. Boil the egg for six minutes and then immediately plunge it into cold water. Finely chop the daikon, season with salt and vinegar and let stand for 10 minutes. Cook the noodles directly in the broth for a few minutes, then drain and divide into two bowls.

Dissolve the miso inside the broth while it is still hot and pour it into the bowls. Garnish with fresh spinach, the vegetables from the broth, sliced raw scallions crispy tofu, half an egg, and seasoned daikon.

Ramen with Seitan and Sesame Seeds

Servings: 4   **Preparation Time: 1 hour**

600 g ramen noodles
1 tablespoon olive or
seed oil
1 clove of fresh garlic
400 g of diced seitan
6 tablespoons of soy
sauce

200 g cabbage
1 pinch of black pepper
20 g sesame seeds

For the broth
1.5 liters of water

2 teaspoons of miso
6 tablespoons of soy
sauce
1 tablespoon of sake
1 tablespoon of garlic
powder
3 slices of fresh ginger

Directions

Start the recipe by taking care of the broth: put water, miso, 3 tablespoons soy sauce, sake, garlic powder, and the ginger slices in a pot. Stir and cook over medium heat until boiling. Remove from heat and strain the broth through a strainer to remove any residue.

In a wok, slowly heat 1 teaspoon of oil and a clove of garlic. Add the seitan pieces that you will have marinated in the soy sauce for about 1 hour. Cook until the meat begins to caramelize, taking care to turn it occasionally for even cooking.

Add the cabbage leaves, season with salt and pepper, and continue cooking for a few minutes. Turn off the heat when the vegetables become tender.

In a separate pot bring water to a boil and cook the noodles. When ready divide them into four bowls, serve them by topping them with the soup and adding the seitan. Garnish with toasted sesame seeds.

Ramen with Curry, Tofu and Coconut Milk

Servings: 2   **Preparation Time: 30 minutes**

300 g ramen noodles

800 ml vegetable broth

180 g Tofu

2 slices of fresh ginger

1 spring onion

1 clove Garlic

6 tablespoons soy sauce

3 tablespoons sesame or olive oil

1 tablespoon Sesame seeds

250 g fresh chiodini mushrooms

200 ml Coconut milk

10 g fresh parsley

For the curry

2 slices of fresh ginger

2 fresh chilies

1 clove of garlic

20 g fresh cilantro

2 tablespoons of tomato paste

½ tablespoon cumin seeds

Directions

First prepare the curry: soak the chilies in a bowl of hot water for about 10 minutes and then drain them, dry them well, cut them in half and remove the seeds. Grind the cumin seeds in a grinder and also chop the ginger and garlic after peeling them. Put chili, garlic, coriander, ginger, cumin, and salt on a cutting board and chop everything with a knife until smooth and very fine. Heat the oil in a small, high-sided nonstick skillet. Add the chopped spices and tomato paste and cook over low heat, stirring constantly with a wooden spoon, for about 5 to 10 minutes or until it begins to smell. Turn off the heat and allow to cool completely.

Boil the mushrooms in plenty of salted water for about 15 minutes, then drain, season with a tablespoon of oil and set aside.

Place cubed tofu in a bowl with minced garlic, ginger, chili and sliced spring onion. Add the soy sauce and let marinate for 30 minutes. Heat a tablespoon of oil in a skillet and brown the tofu on all sides until it forms a crispy crust. Add the sesame seeds when cooked through and set aside.

Heat the broth in a large pot, add the coconut milk and a heaped teaspoon of curry paste. Boil plenty of lightly salted water in a pot and cook the noodles for 3 minutes. Divide the noodles into bowls, add mushrooms and tofu to each serving. Cover with the hot broth. Top the ramen with plenty of chopped parsley and a pinch of pepper.

Vegetarian Ramen with Braised Shiitake

Servings: 4   **Preparation Time: 45 minutes**

600 g ramen noodles
2000 ml vegetable broth
2 tablespoons of seed oil
8 fresh shiitake mushrooms

4 eggs
3 spring onions
3 carrots
150 g cabbage

6 tablespoons of soy sauce
30 g chopped peanuts

Directions

Put a pot on the stove, add oil and brown the mushrooms on all sides to let them take on color and remove the excess water they contain. Add the soy sauce and broth until they are covered about halfway up, this way you will get a "braised" cooking process. Let everything cook with the lid closed for about 30 minutes.

Meanwhile, boil the eggs for 5 minutes in a saucepan full of water. Cut the vegetables into slices. When the mushrooms are cooked, you can remove and slice them. Add the vegetables, roughly chopped, and continue cooking for atri 30 minutes.

After this time has elapsed cook the noodles directly in the broth, for 3 minutes or according to the directions on the package. When ready divide them into bowls, top with the broth, and complete the dish with the mushrooms, soy sauce, and chopped peanuts.

Ramen with Spicy Seitan

Servings: 2   **Preparation Time: 30 minutes**

300 g ramen noodles	3 tablespoons honey	2 tablespoons miso paste
300 g of diced seitan	3 tablespoon sesame oil	400 ml water
700 ml vegetable broth	1 shallot	1 tablespoon sugar
3 tablespoons teriyaki sauce	1 clove of garlic	1 fresh chili pepper
	3 slices of ginger	2 eggs

Directions

Marinate seitan in teriyaki sauce and honey for 30 minutes.

Sauté the shallots, garlic and ginger in a pan in a tablespoon of sesame oil. When everything is cooked, add the miso paste and water. Bring to a boil and cook for 10 minutes. Then add the broth, salt and sugar.

Boil the eggs for about 5 minutes, so you will have the egg white well cooked and the yolk soft, as they are usually eaten in ramen (of course if the soft yolk is not to your liking, you can always cook them a couple of minutes longer). When they are ready, remove them from the water, let them cool, and peel them.

In a small saucepan, bring water to a boil and cook the noodles for 3 minutes or according to the directions on the package. When ready, remove them from the water and set aside.

Pour 2 tablespoons of oil into a skillet; when hot, cook the seitan for 5 minutes.

Divide the noodles into bowls, pour the broth over them, and top the dish with the seitan, halved eggs, and sliced chili.

Vegetarian Hokkaido Ramen

Servings: 2   **Preparation Time: 25 minutes**

300 g ramen noodles
600 ml vegetable broth
2 eggs
4 tablespoons of soy sauce

4 dried shiitake mushrooms
1 clove of garlic, minced
1 onion, chopped
1 chopped carrot

1 chopped leek
50 g fresh spinach
40 g of soybean sprouts
1 tablespoon of sesame seeds

Directions

Soak dried shiitake mushrooms in hot water to soften them.

Bring some water to a boil in a saucepan and cook the eggs inside for 5 minutes, so the white will be cooked and the yolk will remain soft. After this time has elapsed, remove them from the water, peel them and let them marinate in the soy sauce for at least 30 minutes.

Set the broth to heat. Add soy sauce to taste.

Add the chopped vegetables to the broth and cook over medium heat for 5-10 minutes. Add shiitake mushrooms and cook for another 5 minutes.

In a saucepan, bring water to a boil and cook noodles for 3 minutes or according to package directions.

Spread the cooked noodles into bowls and pour the broth over them until they are covered. Decorate with the hard-boiled egg cut in half, fresh spinach, soybean sprouts, and sesame seeds.

Ramen Salad with Tamagoyaki

Servings: 2   **Preparation Time: 25 minutes**

	For the sauce:	Tamagoyaki:
300 g ramen noodles	80 ml rice vinegar	3 eggs
1 teaspoon of seed oil	80 ml soy sauce	1 tablespoon peanut oil
1 cucumber	2 tbsp sugar	½ tablespoon potato starch
12 chopped cherry tomatoes	25 ml sesame oil	
	130 ml water	
	1 tablespoon mustard	

Directions

Fresh and richly flavored ramen salad. Start by pouring about 5 liters of water into a large pot and turn on the heat.

Once the water is boiling, soak the ramen noodles for about 3 minutes. If you are using dry ones, leave them twice as long. Once cooked, run them under running water to remove excess starch, pour them into a bowl along with a drizzle of oil, and turn them with a spoon to prevent sticking.

To make the sauce take all the ingredients, put them in a saucepan and over a low flame slowly bring it to a boil. Once it boils keep stirring until it is reduced by about 2 cm, turn it off and let it cool. Wash and slice the cherry tomatoes and cucumber.

Now you will need to prepare the tamagoyaki. Pour the eggs and potato starch into a bowl and mix until smooth. In a nonstick skillet about 6 inches in diameter pour the peanut oil and heat it. Once hot pour the egg mixture inside, when it starts to cook, turn it over with the help of a spoon and start rolling it gently on itself. Once ready, which will take about 4 minutes, remove it from the heat and cut it into slices of about 2 cm.

Now you are ready to assemble the dish. In a bowl pour the noodles, mix them with the tomatoes and cucumber, add the sauce and tamagoyaki on the side.

Pizza Ramen

Servings: 2   **Preparation Time: 20 minutes**

400 g ramen noodle
250 g of mozzarella cheese

120 g diced tomatoes
3 tablespoons seed or olive oil

4 fresh basil leaves
2 eggs

Directions

In a saucepan, bring water to a boil and cook noodles for 3 minutes or according to package directions. Drain them in a bowl, pour in 2 beaten eggs and mix well.

Pour oil into a baking dish and spread the noodles inside. Sprinkle with a thin layer of mozzarella cheese and the diced tomatoes.

Bake in the oven at 200 °C for about 10 minutes, until the bottom becomes crispy. Garnish with fresh basil leaves and serve while still hot.

Ramen with Peanut Pesto and Tomato

Servings: 2   **Preparation Time: 45 minutes**

300 g ramen noodles
600 ml of vegetable broth
1 tablespoon of tomato paste

2 eggs
250 ml soy sauce
1 spring onion
4 dried shiitake mushrooms

60 g peanuts
1 tablespoon chopped cilantro

Directions

Bring some water to a boil in a saucepan and cook the eggs inside for 5 minutes, so the white will be cooked and the yolk will remain soft. After this time has elapsed, remove them from the water, peel them and let them marinate in plenty of soy sauce for at least 30 minutes. In this dish it is very important that the egg has a strong flavor.

In a saucepan bring water to a boil, cook the noodles inside for 3 minutes or according to the directions on the package. Drain and divide them into bowls.

Add the mushrooms and tomato paste to the basic broth. Turn on the heat and let cook another 15 minutes to let all the flavors blend.

To make the peanut pesto, toast the peanuts in a frying pan for about 5 minutes. Once they start to give off their characteristic aroma, blend them with an electric blender or, better yet, with a hand mortar until they become a smooth paste. If they are too dry and you have difficulty processing them, add a few tablespoons of hot broth.

Pour the soup into bowls until the noodles are coated, add the eggs cut in half and a generous spoonful of peanut pesto. Garnish with chopped cilantro and ring-cut spring onion.

Vegetarian Tantanmen Ramen

Servings: 2   **Preparation Time: 20 minutes**

300 g ramen noodles	*1 tablespoon seed or olive oil*	***For the minced vegetables***
600 ml vegetable broth		
1 fresh chili pepper	*1 clove of garlic*	*2 carrots*
1 tablespoon of sesame paste	*1 shallot*	*1 celery stalk*
	20 g wakame seaweed	*2 onions*
1 tablespoon of soy sauce	*10 g of gari*	*60 g daikon*
	10 g of chives	

Directions

Bring the broth to a boil and season it with chili, sesame paste and soy sauce.

Heat the oil in a frying pan. Add chopped garlic and shallots and cook for about 3 minutes over low heat. Finely chop carrots, celery, onions, and daikon for minced vegetables, add them, and continue cooking for another 5 minutes. Season with soy sauce and chopped chili.

Meanwhile, cook the noodles in a pot of boiling water for 3 minutes or according to the directions on the package.

Divide noodles among bowls, add ground meat, wakame seaweed, and gari. Stir the hot broth vigorously again and pour into the bowls until everything is covered. Garnish with finely chopped chives and serve.

Vegan Ramen

Ramen with Tofu and Mushrooms

Servings: 4   **Preparation Time: 45 minutes**

600 g ramen noodles
2000 ml of vegetable broth
8 fresh shiitake mushrooms
2 tablespoons olive or seed oil

6 tablespoons of soy sauce
400 g tofu
1 spring onion
1 clove of garlic
10 g ginger
3 tablespoons miso

2 teaspoons sugar
4 tablespoons rice vinegar
2 tablespoons fresh cilantro

Directions

First cut the mushrooms into slices and cook them for 3 minutes in a skillet, preferably a thick-bottomed one, in which you will have heated 1 tablespoon of oil. When they are about halfway cooked, season them by adding the soy sauce (about 2 tablespoons).

Set the mushrooms aside and proceed to cut the tofu into cubes and the spring onion into slices. Finely chop the garlic and ginger as well.

In a saucepan, sauté the garlic, ginger, spring onion, and tofu for a few minutes with 1 tablespoon of oil over medium heat, taking care to turn often to prevent burning.

Meanwhile, heat the vegetable broth; once it is boiling, dissolve the miso inside and pour all the liquid into the pot with the tofu.

To make the broth even tastier, take some of the mushrooms, about half, and add them to the broth. Let it cook for 20 minutes to reduce it and intensify the flavor. Meanwhile you can start cooking the noodles in a pot of unsalted boiling water.

Now that all the ingredients are ready in each bowl pour ½ teaspoon sugar, 1 tablespoon soy sauce, and 1 tablespoon rice vinegar. Stir carefully to make a smooth mixture, later add the broth and noodles. Garnish with the mushrooms, thinly sliced spring onion, and a sprinkling of finely chopped fresh cilantro.

Vegan Ramen with Coconut Milk Broth

Servings: 2   **Preparation Time: 2 hours and 15 minutes**

300 g ramen noodles
4 fresh shiitake mushrooms
10 ml maple syrup
1 tablespoon of ginger powder
3 tbsp. soy sauce

400 ml coconut milk
½ onion
200 g tofu
1 tablespoon chopped fresh cilantro
1 tablespoon of seed or olive oil

For the broth
4 liters of water
1 carrot
1 onion
1 celery stalk
3 branches of fresh parsley

Directions

Prepare a vegetable stock by putting coarsely chopped onion, carrot, celery and parsley in 4 quarts of cold water. Turn the heat on low and let it cook for about 2 hours.

Next marinate the mushrooms, as this is a time-consuming preparation. Prepare a sauce by mixing ginger powder, soy sauce and maple syrup evenly. Cut the mushrooms into thin strips, pour the sauce over them and let them sit for about 1 hour.

In a frying pan pour 1 tablespoon of oil, and sauté ½ finely chopped onion for a couple of minutes. Pour in the coconut milk and broth, bring to a boil and let it cook for 30 minutes.

In the meantime, heat another pan, preferably with a thick bottom, pour in the mushrooms and cook them 1 minute per side. Cut the tofu into 2-cm strips (or cubes) and grill it in the same skillet about 2 minutes per side.

Separately, cook the noodles in boiling water, 3 minutes if you are using fresh ones, 6 minutes if you are using dried ones.

When they are ready, compose the dish by pouring the noodles, broth combined with coconut milk, mushrooms and grilled tofu into a bowl. Garnish with chopped cilantro.

Simple Vegan Ramen

Servings: 2   **Preparation Time: 45 minutes**

300 g ramen noodles	*1 shallot*	*1 tablespoon seed or olive oil*
800 ml of vegetable broth	*1 sheet of nori seaweed*	*1 tablespoon miso*
6 shiitake mushrooms	*200 g tofu*	*1 tablespoon paprika*
	1 clove of garlic	

Directions

Soak dried shiitake mushrooms in warm water for about 30 minutes. After this time has elapsed, boil them for 5 minutes, let them cool and cut them into strips.

Cut the shallots into thin rounds, the nori seaweed into strips and the tofu into cubes. Mince the garlic and sauté it in oil, adding the miso and paprika after a minute. Add the vegetable broth.

Cook the noodles in a saucepan of boiling water for 3 minutes or for the time indicated on the package. Drain them well and divide them into two large bowls. Add the broth and garnish generously with shiitake mushrooms, scallions, tofu, and nori seaweed strips.

Vegan Ramen with Spicy Cabbage

Servings: 2   **Preparation Time: 1 hour**

300 g ramen noodles
6 shiitake mushrooms
80 g kombu seaweed
1 onion
3 slices of fresh ginger
1 clove of fresh garlic

2 tablespoons of sesame seeds
150 ml of soy milk
1 tablespoon sesame oil
150 g fresh cabbage

½ tablespoon chili powder
1 tablespoon of soy sauce
1 tablespoon of sake
1 tablespoon mirin

Directions

Soak the mushrooms and seaweed in a cup of hot water (about 2 liters) for 30 minutes. Meanwhile, mince the onion, ginger and garlic. Toast the sesame seeds in a hot pan and pound them in a mortar or electric mixer.

Sauté onion, ginger and garlic together in sesame oil in a skillet for a few minutes.

Bring the water with mushrooms and seaweed to a boil, then remove them so that only the broth remains.

To the onions add the sake, soy sauce and mirin, cook for 5 minutes and add the broth and soy milk.

Chop the cabbage, season it with chili powder and cook it in a skillet for 2 minutes, turning constantly to prevent sticking, once ready set it aside.

Cook the noodles in a saucepan with boiling water for 3 minutes or for the time indicated on the package. Once ready, divide into two bowls, cover with the broth and garnish with the spicy cabbage and crushed sesame seeds.

Quick Vegan Ramen

Servings: 2   **Preparation Time: 40 minutes**

300 g ramen noodles   *1 sheet of nori seaweed*   *About 20 g of soybean*
2 liters of water   *1 tablespoon miso paste*   *sprouts*
6 dried shiitake   *1 fresh leek*   *Soy sauce to taste*
mushrooms

Directions

Soak the shiitake mushrooms in warm water for about 30 minutes and then cut them into slices about 1 cm thick. Cut the nori sheet into strips about 2 x 6 cm.

Boil about 2 liters of water in a saucepan; once it comes to a boil, cook the shiitake mushrooms. After about 10 minutes pour the noodles directly into the water with the mushrooms and cook for 3 minutes or according to the directions on the package. After this time has elapsed remove them from the water, wash them under cold water and set aside.

Dissolve 1 tablespoon of miso in the water and mix thoroughly. Cut the leek into thin slices and rinse the soybean sprouts.

Divide the noodles into bowls, cover them with the still-warm mushroom and miso broth, and complete the dish with the mushrooms, leek, soybean sprouts, and nori seaweed. If you like, you can also add a tablespoon of soy sauce.

Ramen with Basil and Roasted Peanut Pesto

Servings: 2   **Preparation Time: 25 minutes**

300 g ramen noodles
600 ml of vegetable broth
15 g fresh ginger
1 clove of fresh garlic

2 tablespoons seed or olive oil
4 fresh basil leaves
1 tablespoon miso
1 tablespoon of soy sauce

4 fresh shiitake mushrooms
150 g cabbage
60 g peanuts

Directions

Peel the ginger and garlic and cut them into cubes. Heat a tablespoon of oil in a large skillet and pour ginger and garlic inside. After about 10 minutes, add the broth and let it cook for another 15 minutes. Add the miso and soy sauce.

Slice the shiitakes and sauté them in a pan with a tablespoon of oil and the cabbage cut into strips.

In a saucepan, bring water to a boil and cook the noodles for 3 minutes or according to package directions.

In a skillet, toast peanuts for 2 minutes, remove from heat, and grind with a mortar or electric blender until a smooth paste is obtained. Add a tablespoon of broth if the mixture is too dry and difficult to process.

Divide the noodles into bowls, add the mushrooms and cabbage. Complete this wonderful dish with a spoonful of roasted peanut pesto and a few basil leaves.

Cold Ramen Salad

Servings: 2   **Preparation Time: 15 minutes**

300 g ramen noodles   *2 tablespoons soy sauce*   *1 spring onion*
Juice of 1 lime   *½ fresh mango*   *2 carrots*
1 tablespoon sesame oil   *1 chili pepper*   *30 g chopped almonds*

Directions

Cook noodles in boiling water for 3 minutes or according to package instructions, drain and rinse with cold water. Mix the lime juice, sesame oil, and soy sauce in a bowl. Combine the freshly made sauce with the noodles, add the diced mango, chili, sliced spring onion, and carrots cut into sticks.

Let the flavors blend well for 10 minutes, complete with chopped almonds and enjoy this wonderful ramen salad. You can also prepare it the day before and leave it in the refrigerator.

Spicy Ramen with Coconut Milk

Servings: 2   **Preparation Time: 35 minutes**

300 g ramen noodles
800 ml of vegetable broth
100 g fresh mushrooms of your choice
1 clove of garlic
1 spring onion

1 tablespoon of sesame seeds
2 tablespoons olive oil or seed oil
6 wakame seaweed
100 g corn
150 ml coconut milk

2 tablespoons sugar
2 tablespoons of soy sauce
2 fresh chilies
2 tablespoons rice vinegar
30 g bamboo slices

Directions

Thinly slice the mushrooms, garlic, and spring onion. Toast the sesame in a frying pan until golden brown, turning often.

Heat a skillet with a little oil and sauté the bamboo over medium heat for about a couple of minutes (after boiling it for about 10 minutes to soften it). Add the corn and cook for another 3 minutes. Once ready remove and transfer to a bowl.

Add a tablespoon of oil back into the pot and cook the mushrooms for about 5 minutes. Set these aside in another bowl as well.

Bring the broth to a boil by adding the seaweed. After about 10 minutes scoop out most of it with a fork and set aside, then add the coconut milk.

Meanwhile in another small pot filled with boiling water cook the noodles for 3 minutes or according to package directions. Once ready remove them from the water and set aside.

 Pour 1 tablespoon sugar, soy sauce, sliced chili, 1 teaspoon rice vinegar, and sesame oil into each dish and mix with a fork. Fill about ¾ full with the broth and stir again. Add the noodles, then the bamboo, corn, and mushrooms. Garnish with toasted sesame seeds and chili.

Miso Ramen with Coconut Milk

Servings: 2   **Preparation Time: 45 minutes**

300 g ramen noodles
600 ml of vegetable broth
4 shiitake mushrooms
1 onion

2 carrots
1 clove of garlic
2 tablespoons seed or olive oil
2 tablespoons miso paste

150 ml coconut milk
1 spring onion

Directions

Soak the shiitake mushrooms in hot water for 25 minutes. Meanwhile, roughly chop the onion, slice the carrots, peel the garlic and crush it with the side of a knife.

In a saucepan, add 2 tablespoons of oil and sauté the shiitake mushrooms, onions, garlic, and carrots over medium heat until lightly browned. Turn continuously to prevent burning.

Add the broth and miso paste. Let simmer for about 30 minutes. Add the coconut milk, stir well and cook another 5 minutes.

In a saucepan, bring water to a boil and cook the noodles for 3 minutes or according to package directions. Once ready, remove them from the water and set aside.

Divide them into bowls, add broth until covered, and garnish with fresh spring onion cut lengthwise.

Ramen in Sweet and Sour Sauce

Servings: 2   **Preparation Time: 20 minutes**

800 ml of vegetable broth
300 g ramen noodles
1 tablespoon of seed or olive oil
100 g edamame
1 tablespoon of sesame seeds

2 carrots
For the sauce
100 ml water
2 tablespoons of soy sauce
1 tablespoon of cornstarch

1 ½ tablespoons of maple syrup
2 tablespoons of sesame oil
Juice of ½ lemon
1 tablespoon of peanut butter
1 clove of fresh garlic

Directions

To make the sauce, mix water, soy sauce, cornstarch, maple syrup, sesame oil, lemon juice and peanut butter. Also mince the garlic and add it.

Peel the carrots and cut them into thin strips.

In another pot filled with boiling water, cook the noodles for 3 minutes or according to package directions. Once ready remove them from the water and set aside.

Heat some oil in a skillet and sauté the edamame 5 minutes. Add the sauce and cook for a few minutes over medium heat. Then add the noodles and carrot strips to the pan.

Add the broth and stir often until boiling to evenly distribute the sauce among the noodles. When the sauce is creamy and well distributed, remove from the heat; it will take about 5 minutes. Garnish the dish with a handful of toasted sesame seeds.

Ramen with Tofu and Cashews

Servings: 2   **Preparation Time: 2 hours**

300 g ramen noodle
150 g tofu
2 tbsp oil
25 g finely chopped
almonds

For the broth
4 liters of water
3 carrots
1 onion
2 celery ribs
2 medium potatoes

4 slices of ginger
2 tablespoons of soy
sauce
1 sheet of nori seaweed
2 tablespoons miso

Directions

Let's start the recipe by preparing this vegetable broth. Thoroughly wash and chop all the vegetables, it is not necessary to chop them finely, coarse chopping is fine. Pour them into a pot filled with cold water and turn on the heat. Add the ginger and 2 tablespoons of soy sauce.

After about half an hour, add the seaweed and continue cooking for another hour and a half. When the broth is almost ready, dissolve 2 tablespoons of miso in it.

In a frying pan heat a tablespoon of oil, cut the tofu into cubes and sauté for a few minutes. You can also add ginger slices or a hot chili pepper to taste.

Cook the noodles directly in the broth for 3 minutes if they are fresh or twice as long if they are dried.

When they are ready, pour everything into bowls and garnish with the broth and finely chopped almonds.

Vegan Ramen with Miso Broth

Servings: 2   **Preparation Time: 1 hour**

300 g ramen noodles
2 teaspoons miso paste
2 fresh spring onions
4   dried   shiitake
mushrooms
30 g wakame seaweed

1 tablespoon olive or
sesame oil
For the broth
3 liters of water
1 celery stalk
1 carrot

1 leek
1 cabbage
3 tablespoons of soy
sauce

Directions

Soak the shiitake mushrooms in a bowl of warm water for about 30 minutes.

Now take care of the broth. Pour about 3 quarts of cold water into a pot and add roughly chopped carrot, leek, celery and cabbage. Add 3 tablespoons of soy sauce, and cook over low heat for about 1 hour. Remember halfway through cooking to remove and set aside the cabbage.

Also soak the wakame seaweed for 15 minutes.

Now take a frying pan and heat 1 tablespoon of oil in it. When the oil is hot, sauté the finely chopped spring onion, sliced mushrooms and wakame seaweed. Cook for about 5 minutes, turning often to prevent sticking, once cooked set aside.

Add the miso to the broth.

Separately cook the noodles in boiling water for the usual 3 minutes (6 in case you are using dried ones)

In a bowl compose the dish by pouring the noodles first, then the broth, shiitake mushrooms, wakame seaweed and cabbage.

Ramen with Baked Carrots

Servings: 2   **Preparation Time: 1 hour**

300 g ramen noodles
600 ml vegetable broth
1 spring onion
1 clove of fresh garlic
20 g fresh chopped
ginger

2 tablespoons seed or
olive oil
1 tablespoon of soy sauce
4 dried shiitake
mushrooms
1 tablespoon miso paste

3 carrots
150 g tofu
1 teaspoon cornstarch
1 tablespoon chopped
peanuts

Directions

Peel the spring onion and cut it into thin slices; also peel the garlic and mince it. Heat the oil in a fairly large skillet and sauté the spring onion for about 5 minutes, turning occasionally to prevent it from burning. Add the garlic and minced ginger and sauté for 2 minutes.

Add 200 ml of broth and dissolve the fried remnants in the bottom of the pan, helping yourself with a wooden spoon. Incorporate the rest of the broth, soy sauce and dried mushrooms at this point. Bring everything to a boil and let it simmer for about 1 hour with the lid closed. After this time has elapsed, add the miso paste and stir well to incorporate it into the broth.

Once brought to a boil you can cook the noodles directly inside the broth for 3 minutes or according to the directions on the package.

Take the carrots, peel them and cut them into strips. Grease a baking dish with a tablespoon of oil, pour the carrots inside and bake at 230° for 10 minutes.

Cut the tofu into cubes about 1 cm in diameter and mix with 1 teaspoon of cornstarch. Heat oil in a skillet and cook for 8 minutes, turning constantly, until crispy. Distribute the broth and noodles into bowls. Add the tofu, and carrot, garnish with the sliced green parts of the spring onion and a sprinkling of chopped peanuts.

Conclusion

In this book I have sought to delve into the rich and colorful world of ramen, providing you with a wide range of traditional and contemporary recipes to explore.From the classic tonkotsu broth to vegetarian and vegan options, this book has something to offer for every palate.

The techniques and ingredients used in these recipes have been carefully curated to ensure that each bowl of ramen is not only delicious, but also authentic and true to the rich history and cultural significance of the dish.

I hope that I have succeeded not only in providing you with the tools to prepare extraordinary ramen, but also inspired a deeper understanding and appreciation of this beloved dish. Whether you are an experienced ramen enthusiast or a beginner just beginning to explore it, I hope you will find joy and satisfaction in preparing and enjoying these delicious bowls of broth.

If you have enjoyed this book, I invite you to leave me honest feedback, I would greatly appreciate it.

Happy cooking!

Made in the USA
Las Vegas, NV
28 February 2024